what grows?

favorite plants for better yards

what grows
favorite plants for better yards
here?

Volume 1
Locations
Jim Hole

H
HOLE'S

Printed in Canada   5   4   3   2   1

National Library of Canada Cataloguing in Publication

Hole, Jim, 1956-
    What grows here? : favorite plants for better yards / Jim Hole.

Includes index.
Contents: v. 1. Locations.
ISBN 1-894728-02-5 (v. 1)

    1. Gardening. 2. Plants, Ornamental. I. Title.

SB407.H64 2004   635.9   C2004-901319-X

Prepress by Elite Lithographers

Additional photographs used courtesy of Monrovia: p. 105, p. 118, p. 141; Alan Craig/Iseli Inc.: p. 57, p. 205, p. 217

HOLE'S
101 BELLEROSE DRIVE
ST. ALBERT, ALBERTA, CANADA
T8N 8N8

LONE PINE PUBLISHING
10145-81 AVENUE
EDMONTON, ALBERTA, CANADA
T6E 1W9

table of contents

Dedication

...thanks for instilling me with healthy
doses of both curiosity and scepticism.

Acknowledgements

Science—and gardening is certainly that—cannot move forward unless people are willing to ask questions, to challenge conventional wisdom, old myths and even their own preconceived notions. To ask the hard questions takes intellectual bravery, so I'd like to offer my genuine thanks to all the gardeners who have ever asked me a question, whether by e-mail, over the telephone or in person. Your willingness to look for answers has prompted me to ask some good questions of my own and inspired much of my writing. More importantly, it has made my own pursuits in the garden much more rewarding.

FOREWORD

When I started gardening, the answer to the question "What grows here?" seemed pretty straightforward. If someone asked me what to grow in deep shade, I would have given them a hosta and left it at that. But not only are there more shade-tolerant plants to choose from these days, gardeners themselves are getting more sophisticated; today, we want better answers.

I can't recall the first time I heard "What grows here?" simply because the question is so commonplace. Commonplace or not, we should never regard the question too lightly, because how we respond to it reveals much about how we see gardening. Ten years ago, when faced with a particularly troublesome location, I may have simply given up on planting there. But today there are so many more avenues to explore that I find it increasingly difficult to justify surrender.

I believe there's an obvious lesson here: to answer gardening's most enduring question, you've got to keep up with the changes. As gardeners and as human beings, we're always reacting to changes in the environment, our culture, and gardening itself. When we make a conscious effort to learn from these changes, to adapt to new conditions and discover new ways of dealing with those conditions, we grow right along with our gardens.

So, what grows here? In the end, I guess *we* do. And isn't that why we garden in the first place?

–Lois E. Hole

Introduction

A S A PROFESSIONAL GROWER, I've heard people ask "What grows here?" thousands of times. And no wonder. With a seemingly endless list of plant species and varieties to choose from, coupled with a baffling range of location difficulties, you have to narrow down the choices to a manageable selection. This book accomplishes that purpose, listing a wide variety of excellent plants for dozens of different landscaping problems, from the everyday to the unexpected.

In creating *What Grows Here?*, we have not simply chosen plants that will grow in certain locations. Instead, we offer a garden philosophy, a practical approach that we hope will make your garden easier to create, manage and enjoy.

It's not enough to just answer the question "What grows here?". To make the best use of a given space, gardeners should have their ultimate goals in mind. For example, a shrub should not merely hide a drainpipe but should also have a function of its own: to provide attractive foliage, edible berries or delightful fragrance, for example. Similarly, cacti may seem like an obvious choice for a drought-prone hot spot, but if you don't appreciate cacti, this solution would be pointless. If you take full advantage of the advice in this book, you'll learn not just what grows where, but how to develop a solid gardening technique and know when to press on and when to compromise with nature.

We hope you'll make good use of the plant varieties we've suggested. But we hope even more that you'll come away from this book with a better understanding of both your own gardening style and the limitations of landscaping. Sometimes a garden gnome or a slab of concrete is the wisest choice, and it's not giving up to admit it.

"My experiences with gardening—on the farm, in school, in business and in the media—have shown me that if you really want to understand how the garden works, you have to be a sceptic."

A Sceptical Approach

I'm a sceptic. Myths and misconceptions annoy me, not because I'm averse to the occasional flight of fancy, but because I get the most out of life when I can understand its intricacies—in the natural world and human affairs alike. I find that a sceptical eye has served me well in both worlds; but more importantly, I enjoy knowing how things really work, whether the subject is gardening, politics, science or art.

To get the best performance from your plants, you have to know the facts. And if you keep your knowledge up to date, you can take advantage of the latest research, applying expert insight to your own garden.

I keep my gardening knowledge current by reading constantly and visiting (and often speaking at) horticultural trade shows and conventions in Europe and North America. A huge source of learning comes as a result of writing gardening articles for Canadian and American magazines and newspapers, contributing to various Hole's gardening books, answering callers' questions on CBC radio and listening to gardeners. These experiences invariably unearth new knowledge, and I look forward to each new discovery. I've lost count of the number of questions that have led me to investigate new approaches, and sometimes even to modify the way I garden.

My experiences with gardening—on the farm, in school, in business and in the media—have shown me that if you really want to understand how the garden works, you have to be a sceptic. In fact, at our greenhouse,

"When I look at a flower, I can appreciate its beauty—but I'm just as interested in learning what's happening within the plant to produce that incredible colour."

we're pretty much all sceptics. We try out hundreds of new plant varieties every year, putting them through their paces in our gardens. We measure factors like colour intensity, winter hardiness, bloom size and bloom duration to determine whether or not a new variety performs reliably. When anyone tells me a particular plant is a great performer, the first thing I think to myself is, *Prove it.* And I don't mind when customers challenge my recommendations because I know I've done the homework. In fact, one of the pleasures of my job is answering questions and dealing with criticisms: it reinforces my belief that, deep down, most gardeners are interested in the science that makes their gardens work.

Of course, people sometimes ask me leading questions, hoping I'll confirm a favourite gardening myth. I usually have to disappoint them. My purpose is not to punch holes in anyone's ego, but rather to show that some tried-and-true garden solutions are in fact just a waste of time and resources.

Being a sceptic doesn't mean that you have to disbelieve everything you hear, nor that you should discard your grandfather's foolproof method for growing huge tomatoes. It simply means that you need to look at information critically, evaluating each new perspective on its own merits. I never dismiss anything out of hand. Show me the evidence, make a convincing argument, and I'm ready to incorporate new information into my existing body of knowledge.

Nor does a sceptical approach mean that you can't appreciate the wonders of nature. In fact, I think my scepticism has given me a deeper appreciation of my environment. When I look at a flower, I can appreciate its beauty— but I'm just as interested in learning what's happening within the plant to produce that incredible colour. Understanding why some roses release such sweet fragrance or why scaevola thrives in the hot sun fills me with admiration for the incredible diversity and adaptability of life. It also makes me a more capable, more versatile gardener. A sceptical approach is one of my most valuable tools, and it's kept my interest in gardening alive for decades.

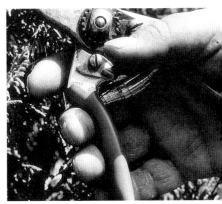

Solid Foundations

Most homeowners have one certain, if vague, goal in mind when they start thinking about their landscape: they want the final product to look *great*. Unfortunately, reaching that goal isn't quite as easy as conceptualizing it. First, you have to know which question you're trying to answer: not just "What grows here?" but "What conditions limit my choices?"

If your plants fail to perform, simple observation may reveal the cause. It may turn out, for instance, that the corner of your yard is drier or shadier than you thought. If everything looks in order, you may need to send some soil to a lab for a soil test. Once you've established the properties of a given location, you'll be in a far better position to determine what grows there.

"The best base on which to build a great garden is a solid foundation of gardening knowledge."

The best base on which to build a great garden is a solid foundation of gardening knowledge. Learn the basic planting techniques and location considerations described on pages 12 to 18. They'll give you a quick but valuable rundown of the most important garden facts. Learning these basics will not only increase your odds of success in general but give you the confidence to experiment. Even M.C. Escher, one of my favourite artists, started with stick figures (or so I like to imagine).

With our plant recommendations, a solid grasp of horticultural facts, your own investigative skills and a little imagination, you'll have an excellent foundation for starting a new garden, renovating an old one or addressing those problem areas.

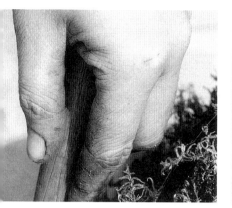

Being a Practical Gardener

Creating a garden that will satisfy your goals demands a little introspection. Your approach to gardening will colour your garden's final look as surely as the plants you choose. Fortunately, there is no right or wrong approach.

At Hole's, I work with a diverse group of horticultural professionals, each with a distinct approach to the garden. Some garden on large lots and acreages, while others have narrow balconies. Some prefer specific categories of plants, while others welcome diversity. Some consider gardening an active part of their lifestyle, while others adopt a low-maintenance approach. Personally, I enjoy investing the time and effort necessary to produce a good-looking overall design for the yard with a few outstanding feature plants, but I don't go overboard. I like to maintain a balance between gardening and my other interests. Knowing that has made me a better gardener.

What kind of gardener are you? Answering that question will help you establish gardening goals. More importantly, understanding your own goals will help you decide which of our suggestions you will find most useful—and which you will ignore.

Find out what kind of gardener you are.
Do you enjoy a shade garden, welcome diversity,
or do you desire a low-maintanence approach?

"Every species and variety has strengths and weaknesses; the same is true of every yard."

"If there's one message I'd like all gardeners to take to heart, it's this: take pleasure in your successes, and be philosophical about failure."

I think of myself as a practical gardener. Every species and variety has strengths and weaknesses; the same is true of every yard. I learned early on to moderate my expectations when experimenting, and to start over when a plant doesn't live up to its promise. Being a practical gardener means being a flexible gardener.

Because of my emphasis on practicality, some might find my advice a little hard-nosed. I don't like to mess around. If a plant isn't working out, I don't hesitate to rip it out and start over, much to the horror of some of my colleagues, who devote months or even years to nurturing struggling plants.

All gardeners, no matter what our specific interests or approaches, have a common goal: we want to grow healthy, good-looking plants. We all make mistakes, have unrealistic dreams and experience failure. I think a practical, realistic approach can mitigate some of these failures, giving us a chance to learn from our mistakes. When you adopt a practical approach, you feel free to change strategies until you find a winning solution.

Surviving Versus Thriving

Not surprisingly, there's a plant out there for almost every location and soil type. But there's a difference between a plant that will just survive in a given location and one that will thrive. If you're willing to experiment, great, you can take some chances, but the key to successful gardening is putting the right plant in the right place.

It's not a mistake to plant something in a less-than-ideal location. Perhaps your apartment balcony doesn't get much sun, but you love tomatoes. Even though tomatoes grow best in full sun, your desire for fresh produce overrides your qualms about growing the plant in partial shade. Maybe you'll get only a few fruits off a plant that has the potential to produce dozens, but that's still more than you would have had if you hadn't tried at all.

That said, it's pointless to let a plant struggle in an unsuitable location, slowly withering away as it struggles to compensate for conditions it hasn't evolved to endure. We've all seen hostas that don't look too bad, considering they're being grown in a fairly sunny spot. But why saddle plants with disadvantages they can barely cope with if you have a better alternative?

A little experimentation is fine, but forcing plants to grow in conditions they simply can't tolerate isn't worth the hassle. Know when to let go of unreasonable expectations.

"Believe it or not, there's a plant out there for almost every location and soil type."

Responding to Change

Over time, plants grow and change. Your favourite rose, a reliable performer for years, eventually gets old and loses its lustre, producing fewer blooms every year. Perhaps your once-perfect garden has regressed over time. Or maybe you're just tired of seeing the same perennials occupying the same spot year after year after year. Spaces evolve and tastes change along with the plants in the garden. Being a practical gardener means responding to change.

Try to anticipate change, rather than simply reacting to it. For instance, if you know your neighbour won't appreciate your plants creeping into his yard, don't plant invasive bamboo or mint anywhere near the property line. Consider dwarf varieties if you know that overhead power lines will one day intersect any tree that grows too tall. And be sure to check out the garden's surroundings from time to time. Neighbouring trees and shrubs grow and change, sometimes enough to make once-sunny areas shady, or vice versa. You may need to change the layout of your garden to compensate.

A garden is not a fixed object, perfect and unchanging once completed. If you're flexible, you'll be able to grow and evolve with your garden and its surroundings.

Substitutions

In this book, we have provided plant selections to meet the needs of particular locations. In most cases we've recommended a specific variety based on our familiarity with its performance. That's not to say another variety of the same plant won't work—as always, don't be afraid to experiment. Use our selections as a guide, but also invest some time in discovering what's available at your local garden centre. If one of our selections isn't available in your area, ask the garden centre staff which plants might work as substitutes.

Garden centres aren't your only resource. Don't neglect the experience and wisdom offered by horticultural societies, books, magazines, the Internet, and your friends, family and neighbours. I've found that gardeners on the whole are generous and informed, willing to share their knowledge and ideas with anyone who's interested. Make use of these valuable resources, but don't let them hold you back from following your own instincts. There are many, many varieties of plants to choose from—as many plants as there are approaches to solving tricky gardening problems. As long as you remain open to new varieties and new ideas, there are few limits to your gardening potential.

"A garden is not a fixed object, perfect and unchanging once completed."

Where Do You Go From Here?

Isaac Newton once said that if he saw farther than others, it was only because he stood on the shoulders of giants. Don't be afraid to look around at your neighbours and friends, and study their choices. What worked? What didn't? What can you learn from the trials and triumphs of others?

I once met a man who successfully grew peaches in Grande Prairie, Alberta, a city with long winters and a short growing season. When he first told me about his unlikely orchard, I was sceptical. But then he described his makeshift greenhouse, which was nothing more than a protective covering of plastic, an unheated oasis that nevertheless protected some healthy and productive trees. I was impressed by his ingenuity, and reminded that with a solid foundation of information and experience, an imaginative gardener can accomplish the seemingly impossible. But that foundation of knowledge is the key: this gardener knew what was possible because he took the time to learn about the cold tolerance of peach trees, determined that maintaining a minimum winter temperature would protect his trees from damage and took steps to create those conditions. Success in the garden, then, could be said to be one-tenth inspiration, four-tenths perspiration and five-tenths preparation.

If there's one message I'd like all gardeners to take to heart, it's this: take pleasure in your successes, and be philosophical about failure. Just as the limitations of art forms can enhance rather than restrict the creative impulse, the limitations in our yards can force us to think harder about what we choose to plant and where we choose to plant it. Embrace the obstacles. You just might discover that every eyesore, every shadowy corner, is an opportunity in disguise.

And if all else fails—if you finally decide that "nothing grows here!"—there's always the garden gnome option.

golden rules

"Location, location, location" isn't just a real estate adage—
for gardeners, these are words to live by. When considering
which plants to choose for a given situation, you must take
several factors into account. If you consider these factors
before sowing or planting, you'll be much more likely to
enjoy success from the very beginning.
Here are my top ten location considerations.

1 Soil Composition

To garden successfully, it's crucial
to have good soil. Soils are complex—and ideally, balanced—
mixtures of clay, silt, sand and
organic matter. Balanced soils
have just the right amount of air
space to allow water to drain at a
moderate pace—slow enough to
allow roots to absorb the moisture,
but fast enough to prevent water-
logging. Most gardeners and farm-
ers refer to such ideal soil as loam.
Of course, "ideal" soil isn't perfect
for all plants; in fact, some do better
in so-called poor soil.

2 Soil pH

Most gardeners know that soil
pH represents the degree of acidity
or alkalinity (also called basicity)
of the soil. What many may not
realize is how pH affects their
plants. Simply put, one of the key
effects of soil pH is determining
how critical nutrients are absorbed.

Soil pH also has a tremendous
effect on soil microorganisms.
Some soil microorganisms convert
compost, manure and other organic
matter into usable nutrients for
your plants. Some of these organisms can't survive in extremely
acidic soil, leaving your plants with
few nutrients to absorb. For most
garden plants, a soil pH between
6.2 and 6.8 is ideal. (Some plants,
of course, do like the extremes:
acidic [lower numbers] for azaleas,
rhododendrons, and blueberries,
and basic [higher numbers] for
gypsophila and Russian olive.)

The Dirt on Soil

Why does soil have such an effect on plants? Because it isn't just a random collection of dust and dirt. Soil is a complex ecosystem of air, water, minerals and organic matter (decayed organisms, usually sold in garden centres as compost, manure or peat moss) and living organisms.

Organic matter is important to plants for several reasons. The decayed portion is a food source for plants. Organic matter helps cement soil particles into tiny aggregates that allow more pore space for roots to grow, as well as allowing water and air to move through the soil more freely. When water can penetrate the soil easily, erosion is reduced substantially.

The addition of organic matter can benefit all kinds of soils. It helps sandy soils hold more water and loosens up heavy soils. Fall is a great time to add organic matter to your soil; you can work it in as you're turning the soil for winter. Just remember that the composition of native soils evolved over thousands of years. Plenty of gardeners have told me that they've added a bag or two of peat moss or compost to their gardens, but have noticed no improvement in their soil. While it's true that a little organic matter is better than none, it takes large amounts of the stuff to enrich truly deficient soils properly. Depending on the size of your garden, it may take many truckloads of compost or peat to make a significant change.

3 Light

Plant leaves are little more than solar energy collectors, using the fuel that sunlight provides for everything from root production to fruit growth. One of the ongoing challenges in the garden is to ensure that plants receive the right amount of sunlight for proper growth.

When customers describe an area of their yard as sunny or shady, we ask how much direct light the area receives and at what time of day. This may sound fussy, but it's actually important because the strength and quality of light changes at different times of day and year.

4 Moisture

Water transports vital nutrients to the "manufacturing centres" of the plant, allowing the production of the fruits, flowers and foliage that we so enjoy. Water also keeps plants cool through transpiration. Water management is crucial to successful gardening.

Observe your yard over the course of a typical season. Some areas will probably be wetter than others, an important consideration when deciding what to plant where.

Is the location bone-dry or perpetually waterlogged? Do your downspouts empty into a bed or do eaves and awnings keep the rain off? Make a rough map indicating the wet and dry zones, and plant accordingly.

5 Zones

Most gardeners are familiar with zone ratings, numbers that indicate the relative mildness of your climate, from the frigid Zone 0 of the far north to the tropical Zone 11 of the southern United States. Most perennials, trees and shrubs have a zone rating, signalling the coldest zone a plant is likely to survive in over winter. Knowing your local zone gives you a basis from which to choose plants, but don't use it as an absolute rule. Zone ratings are largely based on average minimum winter temperatures and factors such as the length of the growing season, soil conditions and fluctuating winter temperatures. They cannot account for highly localized variations.

Every yard has small pockets that are warmer or cooler than their surroundings. These areas are called microclimates, and you can use them to your advantage. My hometown of Edmonton is listed as Zone 3A, but I've successfully grown plants that should, if zone ratings were absolute, have grown only in Zone 6. In any year, there's no way to know exactly which plants will survive in your garden and which ones will not—unless you experiment.

"Observe your yard over the course of a typical season. Some areas will probably be wetter than others, an important consideration when deciding what to plant where."

6 Wind Exposure

Some locations are sheltered; others feel the full force of the wind. Wind dries out branches, leaves and even the soil, and it may be tough on a plant's structure, causing tall stalks to topple and branches to break. Wind can also injure tender new growth and damage or blow off spring blossoms before pollination and fruit set can occur. Especially tall or delicate plants should be planted in a sheltered location, near a fence or wall.

7 Elevation

When considering where to plant, don't forget the third dimension. Even slight elevation changes can affect microclimates. The top of a hill, for instance, is subject to more wind and water run-off than a lower spot, while frost and cool air pool at the bottoms of hills and in even slight depressions in the yard.

8 Available Space

We've all seen landscapes that started off looking just fine but after a few years have become overgrown and out of proportion.

At times we tend to forget that plants grow and change. That spruce tree may be perfect for your yard this year and next, but what about in ten years? A successful landscape plan is one that accounts for mature heights and spreads.

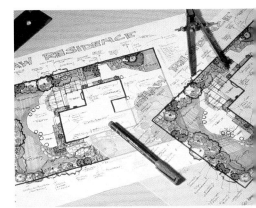

"Any assessment of your yard must include some thinking about how the space is used."

9 Area Use

Any assessment of your yard must include some thinking about how the space is used. It makes no sense to put fragile plants in the children's play area or trees next to the fire pit. Think about the long term—how will the space evolve over time? I, for example, dislike having to duck under branches, so I made sure to plant tall trees well back from the garden path. A good plan acknowledges the fact that as personal needs and desires change, so does the way you use your yard.

10 The Future

Tastes often change over time. If you're getting tired of a plant, even though it looks better than the day you planted it, don't be afraid to remove it. The point of landscaping is to create an environment that you enjoy. New plant varieties are introduced every year. Be willing to acknowledge their benefits and flexible enough to use them to replace old favourites.

"We've all seen landscapes that started off looking just fine but after a few years have become overgrown and out of proportion."

basic planting techniques

The following planting techniques will help to ensure that your plants get their best possible start.

1 Loosen and amend the soil

If you're planting more than one or two plants—a border or bed, for instance—take the time to turn over the entire planting area to a spade's depth. This step loosens the soil and makes planting quicker and easier. Amending the soil at this stage is also easier. A good all-purpose ratio that meets most plants' needs is 80% garden soil to 20% peat moss.

2 Dig a hole for the plant according to its type

For perennials, the planting hole should be twice as wide and as deep as the pot the plant comes in. For trees, shrubs and roses, the hole should be the same height and three times as wide as the rootball. For annuals, the hole should be the same size as the rootball.

If you are adding mycorrhizal fungi (Myke™), sprinkle it onto the soil at the bottom of the hole.

"If you're planting more than one or two plants—a border or bed, for instance—take the time to turn over the entire planting area to a spade's depth."

"Do not remove burlap completely from trees. Open it and set it along the sides of the hole."

3 Remove the plant from its pot

Handling varies, depending on the type of container:

- **Plastic pots** Always remove plastic pots. Gently rough up the sides and bottom of the rootball to promote growth.

- **Fibre pots** Do not remove fibre pots. Cut off the rim and slash the sides. (The fibre pot will gradually decompose.)

- **Balled and burlapped trees** Do not remove burlap completely. Open it and set it along the sides of the hole. (The burlap will gradually decompose.)

Light in this book

Since plants vary in their light preferences, it may be difficult to figure out where to plant them. This confusion leads to plants ending up in the wrong spot. Here's a breakdown of what our light requirements mean.

- **Sun** Plants in this category need full sun all day long for best performance. Fruiting plants, for example, need full sun to produce large yields.

- **Sun to p.m. sun** Plants in this category will bloom and look fine if they receive afternoon sun, from noon until evening.

- **Shade** Shade plants prefer shade all day.

- **Shade to a.m. sun** These plants require cooler, less-intense light. They can tolerate sun from morning until noon, but can't stand hot afternoon sunlight. They will also thrive in dappled light through a tree canopy.

- **Sun or Shade** These plants adapt equally well to sun or shade.

Light requirements are meant to help plants perform to their peak. Plants recommended for full sun, for example, may survive and look fine with only afternoon sun, but they are unlikely to reach their full potential.

4 Plant to the right depth

Put the plant in the hole. The rootball should sit just below ground level. If necessary, refill the bottom of the hole with soil to ensure that the plant is planted to the level it was in its pot. Never plant a tree or shrub deeper than its potted depth. (The one exception to this rule is grafted tender roses: the graft needs to be 8–10 cm below the soil line. If active green growth is visible at the graft, leave a depression in the soil until fall.)

Fill the hole with remaining soil and amendments, and gently pat down the planting area to remove any air pockets. Leave a slight depression around the plant. Stake any tree over 1.5 m tall for one year.

5 Add fertilizer and water in well

Feed the new plants liquid fertilizer (20-20-20). Newly planted trees and shrubs need about 5L of solution for every 30cm of height or spread. If you're using mycorrhizal fungi, water with 20-20-20 fertilizer at half its normal rate.

what comes
next?

The next section of this book is divided into eleven chapters, each covering common landscaping challenges. Here you will find plant listings to cover dozens of specific locations.

"It is often the case that the best solution isn't the one you are consciously looking for."

Each plant listing may include basic information about use, blooms, fragrance, soil requirements, preferred locations, size and light requirements. Plants are listed by common name, series and/or variety in the following categories: Annuals, Perennials, Roses, Vegetables, Fruit and Trees & Shrubs. If you are looking for a specific location or plant use the index to help with your search.

We've selected a broad variety of the best plants for each location and have successfully grown them in Zone 3A. However, if none of our selections is to your taste, or you are having difficulty finding them, be adventurous and choose plants based on growing requirements from another section in this book. You will find in some locations that choices are limited to specific categories.

It is often the case that the best solution isn't the one you are consciously looking for. Don't worry; experiment with your own selections and don't be afraid to arrive at your own answer to the question "What grows here?".

1
Around the
House

…a bridge between your house and your yard…

So many of the questions I am asked relate to houses: what can grow on, around, up and next to them, and how best to grow it. These are insightful questions because houses with nothing planted near them look out of place. They are structures that ignore our ties with nature and the world that surrounds us. I find the answers come easily if I step back, look at the entire environment and explore how the whole home integrates into its surroundings.

I've found that virtually every house has at least four transition zones: one for each side of the house, where the house foundations end and the landscape begins. Creating a bridge between your house and your yard requires some thought, and how you approach the issue reveals much about your gardening style.

At first glance, this interface between the house and the landscape might seem fairly easy to deal with—add a shrub here, a flowerbed there, and you're done. But these zones can actually be particularly challenging. They demand an understanding of the light levels on each side of the house, the dry areas caused by overhangs, and the limitations imposed by downspouts, chimneys, windows and other structures, as well as miscellany such as the effect of light and heat reflect-

ing off stucco, brick or siding. The best solutions usually involve a little creativity.

I purchased a home where the concrete steps, walks and driveway are flush with the foundation almost all the way around the house, limiting my landscaping choices. But as they say, when one door closes, another opens; limits can often enhance creativity. In my situation, container gardening dominates, and to be honest, that's just the way I like it. Using containers allows me to change the plants with ease, not just from year to year but from season to season. During the cooler months of early spring, I fill my containers with pansies. In the summer, I switch to heat-loving calla lilies, verbena or lantana. When fall arrives, I replace these plants with garden mums, and for winter, I put in holiday greenery. Many homeowners prefer more permanence in their landscape, and if this is your aim, you can investigate possibilities from installing a trellis to surrounding your home with perennial beds.

Don't let your home stick out of the ground like the proverbial sore thumb. Integrating our homes into the landscape is a strong first step to acknowledging that humans are part of nature, not apart from it— and to enjoying better gardens. ❧

'Silver Variegated' dogwood thrives in soil that is consistently moist.

The downspouts on the side of my house drain into a bed that, although in a sunny area, remains moist. What grows here?

YOU ARE DEALING with two issues in this situation: moisture and erosion. Fortunately, there are many moisture-loving plants that thrive in soil that remains consistently moist. Take steps to ensure that water pouring out of the downspout at an aggressive rate doesn't displace the soil and expose plant roots. A large, flat rock, stepping stone or mulch placed directly beneath the spout's opening will slow the deluge and preserve the soil.

ANNUALS

Canna Lily 'Pretoria'

Also known as 'Bengal Tiger,' this canna is excellent in mass displays or backgrounds and is used often in waterside plantings. Striking yellow and green striped foliage. Brilliant melon coloured flowers. Height: 1.5m. Sun.

Meadow Foam 'Fried Eggs'

Ideally situated at the front of moist borders as a low, spreading edging. Single blooms are yellow with white tips. Height: 15cm; spacing: 10–15cm. Sun.

Lavatera 'Mont Blanc'

These bushy plants produce pure white, satiny, cup-shaped flowers—very impressive in the garden. Great in mass displays. Height: 60–90cm. Sun.

PERENNIALS

Astilbe
Astilbe japonica 'Deutschland'

A great clump-forming plant for a damp woodland or waterside garden. This heavy feeder produces white plumes in summer. Prefers moist, fertile, organic, alkaline-free soil. Tolerates sun in a boggy site. Height: 45–60cm; width: 40–60cm. Shade to A.M. sun.

Meadow Foam 'Fried Eggs'

Astilbe 'Deutschland'

Canna Lily 'Pretoria'

Downspouts

Common Valerian

Siberian Iris 'Pink Haze'

Common Valerian
Valeriana officinalis

A traditional favourite suitable for mixed borders or natural gardens, preferring moist, fertile soil. Although clump forming and upright in habit, it may require support. Foliage is aromatic with white to pinkish flowers appearing in summer. Height: 1–1.5m; width: 40–80cm. Sun to P.M. sun.

Marsh Marigold
Caltha palustris

Useful in waterside plantings, this plant tolerates full sun if planted in cool, moist soil. Clump forming with kidney-shaped, dark green foliage. Single, yellow-buttercup flowers appear in early spring. Prefers moist, fertile soil. Height: 15–25cm; width: 30–45cm. Shade to A.M. sun.

Siberian Iris
Iris sibirica 'Pink Haze'

One of the least demanding irises, often used in Japanese gardens. A long-lived, clump-forming perennial that thrives in moist conditions. Lavender-pink flowers bloom in late spring. Avoid dry sites. Prefers well-drained, moist, slightly acidic soil. Height: 95cm; width: 30–45cm. Sun to P.M. sun.

Marsh Marigold

TREES & SHRUBS

Dogwood 'Silver Variegated'
Cornus alba 'Argenteo variegata'
A moisture-loving feature shrub for small beds and borders. This beautiful variegated form has bright red bark. Height: 1.5–2m; width: 1.5–2m. Sun to P.M. sun.

Hydrangea 'Pee Gee'
Hydrangea paniculata 'Grandiflora'
Preferring moist soil, this shrub's size can grow much larger depending on climate. Huge, lovely pinkish-white flowers bloom in August. Thin to 5–10 stems for the largest flowers. Height: 1.5–2m; width: 1.5–2m. Sun to P.M. sun.

Larch 'Weeping'
Larix decidua 'Pendula'
The ultimate feature tree for moist sites. Graceful, weeping branches drape over rocks and walls or crawl along the ground. Soft green needles turn glowing yellow and are shed in fall, growing back in spring. Height: training dependent; width: 3–4m. Sun to P.M. sun.

Larch 'Weeping'

Hydrangea 'Pee Gee'

'American Highbush' cranberry will easily disguise a downspout or block it from view, but be sure to take into account its full-grown size.

We have unattractive downspouts on the front and side of our home and want to camouflage them with plants. What grows here?

DISGUISING THE PIPES that drain rainwater from a home's eavestroughs is not difficult and there are many plant selections that will work, depending on the location and height of the downspouts. If you are dealing with a downspout in a narrow side yard, use columnar-shaped plants or trellises and climbers. A top-down solution is to mount a hanging basket near the downspout and fill it with trailing plants. In an area with fewer space restrictions, such as the front of house, there are more choices.

ANNUALS

Nasturtium 'Hermine Grashoff'

An heirloom variety that trails vigourously, providing coverage. Rich, deep orange, fully double flowers cover this plant. All parts of the nasturtium are edible. Trails: 60–90cm; spacing: 25–30cm. Sun to P.M. sun.

Petunia 'Wave Misty Lilac'

Excellent in hanging baskets and containers or as an annual groundcover. Superb weather tolerance. Light lavender, 5–7cm flowers. Height: 15cm; spreads or trails to 120cm. Sun to P.M. sun.

Vinca Ivy 'Green and Gold'
Vinca maculatum
Bright green and gold variegated
foliage with a very vigorous trailing
habit. Great contrast plant. Produces
lilac flowers. Trails to 1–1.5m. Sun to
P.M. sun.

PERENNIALS

Hybrid Clematis
Clematis 'Jackmanii'
A dense, climbing vine that requires
support. Plant all hybrid clematis
against a south or west, heated foundation for winter protection. Grow a
plant or mulch at base to keep roots
cool. Dark purple flowers in early
to late summer. Prefers fertile soil in
a sheltered location. Height: 3–4m;
width: 1–2m. Sun to P.M. sun.

Queen of the Prairie
Filipendula rubra 'Venusta'
Also known as 'Venusta Magnifica,'
this clump-forming variety thrives in
a boggy site and tolerates more sun if
kept moist. Large and fragrant, deep
rose-pink flowers in summer. Prefers
well-drained, organic, moist soil.
Height: 90–150cm; width: 1m. Shade
to A.M. sun.

Vinca Ivy 'Green and Gold'

Petunia 'Wave Misty Lilac'

Nasturtium 'Hermine Grashoff'

Downspouts

Sweet Joe Pye

Sweet Joe Pye
Eupatorium purpureum

A showy perennial that forms a large bush with an upright, clump-forming habit. It contrasts well with evergreens and attracts butterflies. Fragrant, clustered, rose-purple flowers bloom late summer to fall. Prefers moist, alkaline soil. Height: 90–150m; width: 90–100cm. Sun to P.M. sun.

ROSES

'John Davis' Explorer
Hybrid Kordesii

This Canadian introduction can be used as a striking climber and is hardy to Zone 3. Semi-double, medium pink, 8–9cm flowers bloom profusely June through frost with a spicy fragrance. Height: 1.5–2m; spread: 1–2m. Sun.

Clematis 'Jackmanii'

Queen of the Prairie

Cedar 'Holmstrup'

Rose 'John Davis'

TREES & SHRUBS

Cedar 'Emerald Green'
Thuja occidentalis 'Smaragd'
Beautiful emerald-green foliage on
a very compact, pyramidal form that
fits well in tight spaces. Makes a striking feature tree. Height: 3–4m; width:
1–2m. A.M. sun.

Cedar 'Holmstrup'
Thuja occidentalis
Very beautiful when planted in small
groups in shrub beds and great for
hedges and rock gardens. Windburn
resistant foliage on a slow-growing,
pyramidal shape. Height: 1.5m; width:
30–90cm in 10 years. Sun to P.M. sun.

Cranberry 'American Highbush'
Viburnum trilobum
Great shrub for screening. Large, flat
clusters of white blooms in late spring
are followed by masses of edible red
berries. Bright red fall colour. Height:
3–4m; width: 3–4m. Sun to P.M. sun.

Cedar 'Emerald Green'

'Engelmannii' virginia creeper is a good choice for softening vertical lines. A single plant can easily provide wide coverage so be cautious when planting more than one.

Our bungalow has a very wide chimney on the front side. The area receives light all morning and we'd like to plant something that will soften the expanse that the chimney creates. What grows here?

TAKE CARE TO CHOOSE plants that will not outgrow the site and look out of proportion with your home. A combination of plants, rather than one single plant, often looks best when dealing with lower structures. Also, as this side of your home is the most visible, consider how the plant will look in all seasons.

PERENNIALS

Dutchman's Pipe
Aristolochia

Dense, heart-shaped foliage on a climbing vine that requires support. Displays pipe-shaped, maroon and white flowers in early summer. Cut back in fall. Prefers moist, well-drained, organic soil. Height: 3–5m; width: 1–2m. Shade to A.M. sun.

Big Petal Clematis
Clematis macropetala 'Rosy O'Grady'

Produces a lush, pest-free and very hardy screen that requires support. Grow as a climber, groundcover or trail over stonewalls. Do not cut back. Pink-mauve flowers in spring are followed by attractive seed heads. Prefers fertile, well-drained soil and cool roots. Height: 3–5m; width: 1–2m. Sun to P.M. sun.

Virginia Creeper
Parthenocissus quinquefolia 'Engelmannii'

This vine will easily cover a fence, wall or tree stump. Provide support for this vigorous climber. Ivy-like foliage turns brilliant red in fall. Green-white flowers appear in summer followed by blue-black fruit. Do not cut back in fall. Prefers fertile, well-drained soil. Height: 5–10m; width: 2–3+m. Sun or shade.

ROSES

'Fruhlingsmorgan'
Hybrid Spinosissima

Also known as 'Spring Morning,' this hardy shrub makes a lovely climbing rose. Single, 6cm flowers are cherry pink with a soft yellow centre and have an unusual fragrance. Blooms late spring to early summer. Height: 1.5–2m; spread: 1–1.2m. Sun.

TREES & SHRUBS

Burning Bush 'Compact'
Euonymus alatus 'Compactus'

Also known as 'Dwarf,' this rounded shrub with flaming-red fall colour is attractive in borders and small shrub beds. Shear and shape for a more formal appearance. Height: 1.5–2m; width: 2–3m. Sun or shade.

Cedar 'Woodwardii'
Thuja occidentalis

A globe-shaped form that helps soften a large expanse. This hardy cedar holds its dense, deep green foliage to the ground and looks great in large beds and rock gardens. Best shaped annually. Height: 2m; width: 2–3m. Sun to P.M. sun.

Rose 'Fruhlingsmorgan'

Burning Bush 'Compact'

Big Petal Clematis 'Rosy O'Grady'

Dutchman's Pipe

Canary bird vine is a climbing annual that is easily capable of reaching a second storey.

I have a two-storey fireplace at the side of my house that I would like to disguise using plants. It is hot and sunny on this brick wall, so I need heat-tolerant plants. What grows here?

AS YOUR FIREPLACE WALL is situated at the side of your home, select plants that will allow for easy passage when full grown. Choose compact, columnar forms or climbers and avoid the common mistake of planting shrubs or evergreens that will grow to block access through the area.

ANNUALS

Canary Bird Vine

This heat-loving, fast-growing annual vine requires support. It produces masses of tiny, yellow, 1cm, orchid-like flowers. Height: up to 4m; spacing: 25–30cm. Sun.

Sunflower 'Soraya'

A sun and heat-loving annual that produces many, rich golden-orange, 10–15cm blooms. Makes an excellent cutflower. Height: 1.75m; spacing: 45–60cm. Sun.

FRUIT

Grape 'Beta'
Vitis

An attractive alternative to the usual vines, this hardy grape produces heavy yields of blue, 1cm fruit in late August and early September. Harvest the fruit for juice and jelly. Requires support. A great cross pollinator for other grapes. Height: training dependent. Sun.

PERENNIALS

Common Hops
Humulus lupulus

This vigorous climbing vine covers a large area and requires a strong support. Cone-like, green female flowers in summer. Cut back in fall. Prefers well-drained, organic, moderately fertile, moist soil. Height: 4–6m; width: 2–3+m. Sun to P.M. sun.

Dark Eye Sunflower
Helianthus atrorubens

Valued for its upright habit, height and late season blooms. Deep yellow flowers with dark red centres appear in late summer. Prefers fertile, well-drained soil but will tolerate dry soils. Height: 90–120cm; width: 60–90cm. Sun to P.M. sun.

Dark Eye Sunflower

Sunflower 'Soraya'

Common Hops

Fireplaces

Hybrid Clematis 'Ville de Lyon'

False Sunflower
Heliopsis helianthoides

Suitable for any mixed border where
height is required. Clump-forming.
Single or double, golden-yellow flowers
in mid summer to fall make excellent
cutflowers. Prefers fertile, well-drained,
moist, organic soil. Height: 1–1.5m;
width: 60cm. Sun.

Hybrid Clematis
Clematis 'Ville de Lyon'

A dense, climbing vine that requires
support. Plant all hybrid clematis
against a south or west, heated foundation for winter protection. Grow a
plant or mulch at base to keep roots
cool. Bright crimson flowers bloom in
summer. Prefers fertile soil in a sheltered location. Height: 3–3.5m; width:
1–2m. Sun to P.M. sun.

False Sunflower

Rose 'Louis Jolliet'

ROSES

'Louis Jolliet' Explorer
Hybrid Kordesii

A versatile rose that can be grown as a shrub or climber. Double, medium pink, 7–8cm flowers bloom all summer with a spicy fragrance. Hardy to Zone 3. Height: 100–150cm; spread: 90–150cm. Sun.

TREES & SHRUBS

Juniper 'Skyrocket'
Juniperus scopulorum

Perfect for formal gardens and small yards. Striking silvery-blue foliage on an extremely narrow, upright form. Height: 4–5m; width: 45–60cm. Sun.

Ornamental Crabapple 'Thunderchild Columnar'
Malus x *pumila*

This unique columnar form has many uses in the landscape: plant a few in a row for a narrow screen or use to highlight entrances, driveways, and sunny side yards. Displays deep burgundy-purple foliage and abundant pink blooms in spring. Height: 3m in 5–6 years; width: 30–60cm. Sun.

Juniper 'Skyrocket'

'William Baffin' and 'John Cabot' roses can be easily trained to climb on railings and trellises.

We have an older home that has unattractive, poured concrete steps with a set of wrought iron railings. There is a sunny area for planting next to the steps. What grows here?

THERE ARE MANY PLANTING OPTIONS that offer an attractive way to highlight a front entrance while camouflaging a perfectly functional, although dated, railing that extends upward to the eaves. Try hanging baskets or a planter mounted on the rail; also consider climbing or tall, narrow plants.

ANNUALS

Sweet Pea 'Gwendoline'

Huge, lilac pink, wavy flowers bloom with amazing scent atop strong stems—perfect for cutflower bouquets. Very showy. Height: up to 2m. Sun.

Marigold 'Jubilee Diamond'

Excellent in backgrounds or used as an annual hedge. Strong, sturdy stems support lemon yellow, 8cm, fully double flowers. Height: 75–80cm; spacing: 30–35cm. Sun.

Petunia 'Easy Wave Cherry'

Excellent in hanging baskets or patio pots. Spreading and mounding growth covered in hot cherry rose, 6cm flowers. Extremely weather tolerant. Height: 20–30cm; spreading to 75cm. Sun to P.M. sun.

Petunia 'Easy Wave Cherry'

Sweet Pea 'Gwendoline'

Marigold 'Jubilee Diamond'

Daylily 'Hyperion'

PERENNIALS

Daylily
Hemerocallis 'Hyperion'

A classic with grass-like, clump-form-ing foliage. An extended bloomer—fragrant flowers last longer than a single day. Lemon yellow flowers appear in mid season. Prefers moist, fertile, well-drained soil. Height: 95cm; width: 45–90cm. Sun to P.M. sun.

Delphinium 'Blue Jay'
Delphinium

Delphinium's upright habit benefits from a wind-sheltered location. Divide every 3–4 years and cut back after flowering to promote re-blooming. A heavy feeder that may require staking. Spiked, dark blue flowers with dark eyes bloom in summer. Prefers moist, fertile, well-drained soil. Height: 1–1.5m; width: 75–90cm. Sun to P.M. sun.

Double Hollyhock
Alcea rosea

This well-loved, upright biennial is available in assorted colours. Spiked, double, ruffled flowers bloom in sum-mer. Prefers fertile, well-drained soil. Height: 1–2m; width: 60–90cm. Sun to P.M. sun.

Delphinium 'Blue Jay'

Double Hollyhock

Peony
Paeonia 'Dandy Dan'

A compact, clump-forming peony that blooms early and has thicker stems that hold up better to adverse weather conditions. Plant eyes 5cm deep or less. Semi-double, dark red flowers appear in spring. Prefers moist, acid-free, fertile, well-drained soil. Height: 60–65cm; width: 60–90cm. Sun to P.M. sun.

ROSES

'John Cabot' Explorer
Hybrid Kordesii

A stunning, disease-resistant climbing rose that is hardy to Zone 2. Double, medium red, 7–8cm flowers bloom repeatedly early summer to frost, producing a light fragrance. Height: 3m; spread: 1.5–2m. Sun.

'William Baffin' Explorer
Hybrid Kordesii

Producing large clusters of up to 30 roses, this hardy-to-Zone 2 climber blooms all summer. Semi-double, red-pink with yellow centres, 6–7cm flowers are lightly fragrant. Height: 2–3m; spread: 1.5–2m. Sun.

Lilac 'Dwarf Korean'

TREES & SHRUBS

Lilac 'Dwarf Korean'
Syringa meyeri 'Palibin'

This small, compact lilac does not sucker and makes a nice feature or a lovely hedge. Red-purple buds open to pink-purple, fragrant blooms in late spring. Height: 1–2 m; width: 1.5–2m. Sun to P.M. sun.

Peony 'Dandy Dan'

Rose 'William Baffin'

Rose 'John Cabot'

Steps & Stairs

Using lower-growing plants like 'King of Hearts' Pacific bleeding heart in front of basement windows still allows light to enter.

I have large window wells around my basement windows with flowerbeds surrounding them. I would like to have plants in these beds, but not block the light coming into the house. What grows here?

EXTEND YOUR FLOWERBEDS past the sides of the window wells and place tall and narrow columnar plants at each side and progressively lower-growing plants towards the area directly in front of the window.

ANNUALS

Lobelia, Palace Series
This short, fragrant plant is useful at the front of borders and in planters. 1cm flowers in a selection of colours and bronze-green foliage with a mounding growth habit. Height: 7–10cm; spacing: 15–20cm. A.M sun to P.M. sun.

Pansy, Whiskers Series
Excellent garden performance and frost tolerance highlights this series. 6–7cm flowers with a unique cat-face pattern available in different colour combi-nations. Height: 15–20cm; spacing: 20–25cm. Sun to P.M. sun.

PERENNIALS

Daylily
Hemerocallis 'Stella de Oro'
A short, clump-forming daylily that produces golden-yellow flowers con-tinuously summer to fall. Its fragrant flowers last longer than a single day. Prefers moist, fertile, well-drained soil. Height: 30cm; width: 30–60cm. Sun to P.M. sun.

Greyleaf Cranesbill
Geranium cinereum 'Ballerina'

An undemanding and long-lived plant with attractive evergreen, grey-green foliage. Produces red-veined, lilac-pink flowers with red centers in late spring to summer. Prefers well-drained soil. Height: 10–15cm; width: 20–30cm. Sun to P.M. sun.

Pacific Bleeding Heart
Dicentra 'King of Hearts'

A pretty, clump-forming perennial with fern-like foliage. Use as a groundcover in a woodland garden. Dark rose flowers appear in spring to summer. Avoid hot and windy sites. Prefers moist, well-drained, fertile, organic soil. Height: 15–25cm; width: 30–45cm. Shade to A.M. sun.

ROSES

'Charles Albanel' Explorer
Rugosa

This Explorer rose makes a stunning groundcover and is hardy to Zone 1. Semi-double, medium red, 7–9cm flowers are borne in clusters all summer. Produces a light fragrance. Height: 30–60cm; spread: 90cm. Sun.

Daylily 'Stella de Oro'

Pansy 'Whiskers Purple-White'

Rose 'Charles Albanel'

Greyleaf Cranesbill 'Ballerina'

Lobelia 'Palace Blue'

Windows

Windows

The trailing habit of 'Galleria Pink Punch' geraniums makes it perfect for window boxes.

I have a raised brick planter under my west-facing front window. It is narrow and always seems to be dry. What grows here?

ANNUALS AND SMALL PERENNIALS or shrubs are the best choices for this location. The most immediate consideration, however, is with soil quality and volume. Most gardeners fill these types of raised planters once with garden soil and never refresh or add to it once it has settled. It tends to dry out quite quickly in sunny conditions. Supplement the existing soil with a good quality potting mix and be prepared to water regularly.

ANNUALS

Dichondra 'Silver Falls'

A vigorous and cascading habit makes this plant a great choice for hanging baskets, mixed planters, or as an annual groundcover. Small, rounded, shiny silver leaves. Heat and drought tolerant. Height: 5–7cm; trails to 120cm. Sun to P.M. sun.

Gazania, Daybreak Series

A heat loving annual that thrives in dry borders and rock gardens. 10cm, daisy-like flowers available in stunning individual colours and as a mixture. Height: 20–25cm; spacing: 15–20cm. Sun.

Geranium, Galleria Series

This series displays an outstanding mounding and trailing habit and is very effective cascading over container edges. This heat-tolerant, trailing zonal geranium is available in many colours. Height: 30-35cm. Sun to P.M. sun.

Kenilworth Ivy
Cymbalaria muralis

Tiny, round, glossy foliage with a trailing growth habit provides excellent contrast in hanging baskets and containers. Can be grown as an annual groundcover. Produces small, lilac flowers. Trails to 60–90cm. Shade to A.M. sun.

Dichondra 'Silver Falls'

Gazania 'Daybreak Garden Sun'

Kenilworth Ivy

Windows

Lantana, Landmark Series

Although Lantana may not look like much at the bedding out stage, it goes on to provide stunning mass displays in planters and hanging baskets. 'Rose Glow' displays rosy pink to glowing yellow, dense, clustered flowers that attract hummingbirds. Highly fragrant foliage. Heat and drought tolerant. Height: 35–50cm; spreads to 60cm. Sun.

PERENNIALS

Common St. John's Wort
Hypericum perforatum

A good groundcover for sharply draining, moist, moderately fertile soil. Produces bright yellow flowers in summer and red foliage in fall. Height: 60–90cm; width: 45–60+cm. Sun.

Creeping Baby's Breath
Gypsophila repens

A drought-tolerant, mat-forming plant with a creeping habit. Use in a rock garden or a raised bed. White flowers appear in late spring to early summer. Prefers sharply-drained, deep, alkaline soil—avoid winter wet. Height: 15–20cm; width: 30–50cm. Sun to P.M. sun.

Russian Stonecrop

Lantana 'Landmark Rose Glow'

Creeping Baby's Breath

Russian Stonecrop
Sedum kamtschaticum

A clump-forming succulent, tolerant of poor soils and dry periods. Makes a good groundcover. Yellow flowers appear in summer. Prefers well-drained, moderately fertile soil. Height: 20–25cm; width: 30cm. Sun to P.M. sun.

Silver Mound
Artemisia schmidtiana 'Nana'

Wonderful for rock gardens, borders, edging and excellent as an accent plant. Will withstand hot, dry locations. Do not fertilize. Prune back hard in spring. Silky-soft, silver-grey foliage is mound forming. Thrives in well-drained, alkaline, poor, dry soil. Height: 8–10cm; width: 30cm. Sun to P.M. sun.

TREES & SHRUBS

Barberry 'Golden Nugget'
Berberis thunbergii 'Monlers'

A dwarf, slow-growing accent plant that provides contrast in borders, shrub beds and rock gardens. Berries are striking in winter. Newest growth is dense and a deep orange maturing to golden yellow. Height: 30cm; width: 45cm. Sun.

Barberry 'Golden Nugget'

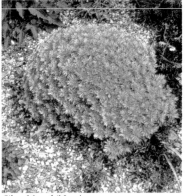

Silver Mound 'Nana'

Common St. John's Wort

Ostrich fern's beautiful arching fronds add texture and a sense of movement, filling a shady, moist area.

Our large front window sits about 1m above the ground. The area in front of it is shady, always moist, never seeming to dry out. What grows here?

Moist, shady sites pose little difficulty, as long as you choose the right plants for the location. Think of the area as a forest floor, well suited to ground-hugging and slightly taller plants that thrive in shade and moist soil conditions.

ANNUALS

Begonia, Non-Stop Series
Bright clear colours and stunning, large, double flowers make this series a winner. Height: 20–25cm; spacing: 15–25cm. Shade to A.M. sun.

Coleus, Wizard Series
An excellent accent plant with superb combinations of multicoloured leaves that really pop in a shady spot. Great in hanging baskets, containers or flower-beds. In northern gardens, it does best

above ground in containers where the soil is warmer. Often grown in mass displays. Height: 25–30cm; spacing: 20–25cm. Shade.

PERENNIALS

Hosta
Hosta 'Abiqua Drinking Gourd'
Hostas are quite tolerant of deep shade, but grow best in open shade with dappled sunlight. Clump-forming habit with big, cupped, thick, blue-green

foliage. Blooms in summer. Thrives in moist, fertile, well-drained, organic, slightly acidic soil. Height: 60cm; width: 1m. Shade to A.M. sun.

Ostrich Fern
Matteuccia struthiopteris

A very popular native fern that is vigorous and colony forming. Beautiful, arching fronds resemble ostrich plumes. Protect from wind. Moist, organic, well-drained, acidic soil. Height: 1–1.5m; width: 60–75cm. Shade to A.M. sun.

TREES & SHRUBS

Cranberry 'Dwarf European'
Viburnum opulus 'Nanum'

Excellent for low hedges, small beds or borders. Deep green foliage on a very compact, small shrub. Height: 60–90cm; width: 90–150cm. Sun or shade.

Euonymus 'Golden Prince'
Euonymus fortunei

A very nice accent plant and probably the hardiest of the wintercreeper euonymus. New growth is a showy, bright yellow on a vigorous, mounding form. Must have snow cover. Height: 60cm; width: 90–100cm. Sun or shade.

Euonymus 'Golden Prince'

Hosta 'Abiqua Drinking Gourd'

Coleus 'Wizard Mix'

Begonia 'Non-Stop Yellow'

Cranberry 'Dwarf European'

Windows

Planting directly beneath a cantilevered window is a real challenge, but the area in front of or beside it offers better opportunities.

I have a large, cantilevered window that overhangs a flowerbed in my backyard. The area directly beneath it is dry and although there is sun, the closer you go towards the house, the shadier it gets. What grows here?

DON'T WORRY ABOUT PLANTING directly under the extension. The same effect can be achieved by planting taller plants in front of this space where light and access to moisture is better. If conditions prevent planting in the ground, consider containers or a raised planter placed in front of the cantilever.

ANNUALS

Kochia 'Childsii'

Soft, feathery, bright green foliage and a uniform bushy growth habit provide lots of coverage. Good choice for backgrounds. Turns a brilliant red in fall. Heat and drought tolerant. Height: 60–90cm. Sun.

Marigold, Antigua Series

Available in a mix or individual showy colours, this African marigold has a compact, even growth habit that is great in borders. 8cm, double flowers are weather tolerant. Height: 20–25cm; spacing: 20–25cm. Sun to P.M. sun.

Zinnia, Peter Pan Series

A very colourful addition to borders that is best directly seeded into the garden. Large, 10cm, semi-double and double flowers available in many vibrant individual colours and a mix. Height: 25–30cm; spacing: 15–20cm. Sun.

Daylily 'Houdini'

Kochia 'Childsii'

Windows

Marigold, Antigua Series (front) & Marigold, Jubilee Series (back)

Windows

PERENNIALS

Bigroot Cranesbill
Geranium 'Johnson's Blue'

Good for use as a groundcover to control weeds, even in dry shade. Displays a spreading habit with aromatic foliage and good fall colour. Produces lavender blue flowers in early summer. Prefers well-drained soil. Height: 30–45cm; width: 60–75cm. Sun or shade.

Blue Oat Grass
Helictotrichon sempervirens

A tall, clump-forming grass with blue, spiky foliage and arching, tan seed heads in summer. Provides nice contrast with other perennials or shrubs, particularly those with purple, yellow or silver foliage. Prefers fertile, well-drained, alkaline soil—avoid winter wet. Height: 90–100cm; width: 60cm. Sun to P.M. sun.

Common Beardtongue
Penstemon 'Prairie Dusk'

A graceful upright plant with tubular, red-violet flowers on tall spikes that are irresistible to hummingbirds. Blooms in late spring to late summer and is drought tolerant, although it prefers fertile, well-drained soil. Height: 45–60cm; width: 45–60cm. Sun to P.M. sun.

Daylily
Hemerocallis 'Houdini'

Arching foilage and a clump-forming habit provide coverage. Produces violet flowers with cream eye in July and is considered an extended bloomer—flowers last longer than a single day. Prefers moist, fertile, well-drained soil. Height: 60cm; width: 45–75cm. Sun to P.M. Sun.

Caragana 'Russian Globe'

Potentilla 'Mango Tango'

Blue Oat Grass

Common Beardtongue 'Prairie Dusk'

Rose 'Purple Pavement'

White Single Baby's Breath

White Single Baby's Breath
Gypsophila paniculata
An upright form with single, white flowers in summer that are good cut and dried. Use in a mixed border. Tolerant of a dry location but dislikes being moved. Prefers sharply-drained, deep, alkaline soil—avoid winter wet. Height: 90–120cm; width: 90–100cm. Sun to P.M. sun.

Roses

'Purple Pavement' Pavement
Hybrid Rugosa
A tough and hardy rose, also known as 'Rotesmeer,' which blooms summer to frost. Semi-double, purplish red with yellow eye, 6–8cm flowers present in small clusters with a light fragrance. Height: 75–90cm; spread: 100cm. Sun.

Trees & Shrubs

Caragana 'Russian Globe'
Caragana frutex 'Globosa'
A nice, tight rounded form, perfect for rock gardens and small spaces. Medium to light green foliage on a slow-growing and extremely hardy plant. Height: 60–90cm; width: 60–90cm. Sun.

Potentilla 'Mango Tango'
Potentilla fruticosa
This variety, bred in Manitoba, is great for hedges, borders and shrub beds. Abundant yellow-orange blended blooms in summer. Height: 60–75cm; width: 60–75cm. Sun.

Shrubs like 'Dwarf European' cranberry deal well with the dry conditions found around the foundations of your home.

The bed running along the foundation at the front of our home faces north and is under eaves that extend outward about 60cm, so it's essentially dry shade. What grows here?

CONTRARY TO POPULAR belief, deep eaves are not always responsible for dry soil in a foundation bed. It often has to do more with how the prevailing winds drive rainfall. By improving the soil, watering regularly and mulching the soil, you can increase your chances of success and expand the available plant choices.

ANNUALS

Nolana 'Sky Blue'
This little plant with a creeping habit tolerates wet or dry soils. Excellent in rock gardens, as an edging or annual groundcover. White centred, sky-blue, petunia-like flowers. Height: 25cm; spacing: 25–30cm. Sun or shade.

PERENNIALS

Lady's Mantle
Alchemilla mollis
A versatile plant that prefers well-drained soil, is drought tolerant and does quite well in dry shade. Clump-forming, slightly lobed leaves hold raindrops and look especially pretty after rain. Produces lime-green flowers in late spring to fall that make long-lasting cut flowers and dry well. Height: 45cm; width: 45cm. Sun to P.M. sun.

Longleaf Lungwort
Pulmonaria longifolia
'Bertram Anderson'

Lungworts are very tough plants used as a groundcover for woodland gardens or border edging. Clump-forming, silver spotted foliage. Produces deep violet-blue flowers in spring. Prefers fertile, well-drained, organic soil. Height: 20–30cm; width: 45–60cm. Shade to A.M. sun.

TREES & SHRUBS

Cranberry 'Dwarf European'
Viburnum opulus 'Nanum'

Excellent for low hedges, small beds or borders. Deep green foliage on a very compact, small shrub. Height: 60–90cm; width: 90–150cm. Sun or shade.

Lady's Mantle

Flowering Raspberry
Rubus odoratus

Great for screening or as a background, especially in full shade. Large showy purple blooms in early summer. Height: 2–3m; width: 2–3m. Shade.

Nolana 'Sky Blue'

Flowering Raspberry

Longleaf Lungwort 'Bertram Anderson'

Foundations

Plants like purple coneflower can withstand the radiated heat and reflected light from white siding.

The siding on our home is white and the front yard faces south. We'd like to camouflage the grey foundation with plants, but everything we choose seems to fry to a crisp. What grows here?

Although your white siding provides a neutral background for planting, it is reflecting sunlight onto an already hot location. Plants placed here will have to be especially heat tolerant, but you can reduce the glare by mounting lattice work or a trellis in front of the siding, up which heat loving vines can grow, in turn reducing the glare for other plants grown in front of them.

ANNUALS

Mandevilla 'Alice Dupont'

This tropical climbing beauty thrives in a hot location, provided it is given lots of water. Glossy dark green foliage and bright rose-red, large, hibiscus-like flowers are stunning. Grow on a trellis. Can be overwintered in a very sunny spot in the house. Height: 1–1.5m. Sun.

Cleome, Sparkler Series

Great in tall borders or in backgrounds. Spider-like, clustered flowers bloom in shades of blushing pink to white. Heat and drought tolerant. Height: 90cm; spacing: 30–40cm. Sun to P.M. sun.

PERENNIALS

False Indigo
Baptisia australis

Lupine-like, blue flowers in late-spring to early summer on an upright form. Thrives in well-drained, sandy, deep poor soil. Height: 60–90cm; width: 60–90cm. Sun.

Mandevilla 'Alice Dupont'

False Indigo

Cleome 'Sparkler Blush'

Foundations

Barberry 'Rose Glow'

Plain's Prickly Pear Cactus

Goldenrod 'Crown of Rays'

Goldenrod
Solidago 'Crown of Rays'

Does best in poor to moderately fertile soils in warm, sunny spots. Does not cause hay fever. Has an upright habit and produces large, flat-headed, bright yellow flowers in late summer to fall that are superb for fresh or dry bouquets. Prefers sandy, well-drained soil. Height: 45–60cm; width: 30–45cm. Sun.

Plain's Prickly Pear Cactus
Opuntia polyacantha

A southern Alberta native with a clump-forming prickly pads and a spreading habit. Thrives in a hot, dry site, be it rock garden, raised bed, trough or stone wall. Yellow flowers in early summer. Needs sharply-drained, gritty, moderately fertile soil—avoid winter wet. Height: 8–15cm; width: 30–60+cm. Sun.

Purple Coneflower
Echinacea purpurea

A wonderful heat-tolerant perennial that is drought tolerant once established. Clump-forming in habit. Reflexed, purple flowers bloom summer to fall attracting butterflies and making long-lasting cutflowers. Prefers well-drained soil. Height: 90–150cm; width: 45cm. Sun to P.M. sun.

TREES & SHRUBS

Barberry 'Rose Glow'
Berberis thunbergii var.
atropurpurea
Extremely tolerant of heat, this
barberry is especially striking planted
en masse or used as a contrast shrub.
Yellow blooms in May and June are
followed by red fruit. Unique rose-pink
mottled leaves mature to deep purple
and in fall turn pink-purple. Height:
90–100cm; width: 60–90cm. Sun.

Broom 'Cyni'
Cystis nigricans
Stunning in bloom and great for a hot
and dry location. Showy yellow blooms
on a compact form. Prune in spring to
encourage bloom clusters. Height: 1m;
width: 1m. Sun.

Pine 'Mops'
Pinus mugo
An ideal small pine for shrub beds and
very heat tolerant. Naturally dense in
habit and slow growing—doesn't need
pruning to maintain shape. Height: 1m;
width: 1m in 15–18 years. Sun to P.M.
sun.

Spiraea 'Anthony Waterer'
Spiraea japonica
A heat tolerant shrub with unusual
bluish foliage that contrasts well with
blooms. Dark pink blooms appear in
mid summer for 3–5 weeks. Height:
90–100cm; width: 90–100cm. Sun to
P.M. sun.

Spiraea 'Anthony Waterer'

Broom 'Cyni'

Pine 'Mops'

Foundations

Entrances

Hanging baskets filled with ivy geraniums like 'Guillou Mauve' help soften the edges of a portico.

My home has a long portico above the front door, supported by two columns. I would like to grow plants under this overhang and perhaps on it. What grows here?

THERE IS LITTLE LIGHT, reflected or otherwise, directly under a portico. Horticulturists call this deep shade. Try growing containers of interesting plants normally enjoyed indoors as houseplants and be vigilant about watering. The light available on the columns would be more substantial. Grow vines on them or mount hanging baskets for a more welcoming entrance.

ANNUALS

Asparagus Fern
Showy, deep green, tapered foxtail-like spikes. Tolerant of heat, drought and wind. Height: up to 45cm. Shade.

Begonia, Non-Stop Series
Bright, clear colours and stunning, large, double flowers make this series a winner. Height: 20–25cm; spacing: 15–25cm. Shade to A.M. sun.

Boston Fern
Place this fern, traditionally grown as a houseplant, in a shady spot protected from wind and keep well watered. Graceful arching green fronds. Shade.

Ivy Geranium 'Guillou Mauve'
Large and attractive, mauve flowers and a cascading growth habit create tremendous displays in windowboxes

and hanging baskets. Height: 20–25cm. Sun to P.M. sun.

Oxalis 'Sunset Velvet'
Oxalis vulcanicola

An ideal accent plant. Yellow, 1cm, bell-shaped flowers on red stems with copper-maroon foliage. Has an interesting mounded, semi-trailing habit. Height: 15–20cm; spacing: 20cm. Shade.

PERENNIALS

Scarlet Trumpet Honeysuckle
Lonicera x *brownii* 'Dropmore Scarlet'

This easy to grow vine requires support to climb. The orange-scarlet flowers that bloom in early summer to fall attract hummingbirds. Flowers are followed by red berries. Do not cut back in fall. Prefers well-drained, organic, moist soil but is somewhat drought tolerant. Height: 3–4m; width: 1–2m. Sun to P.M. sun.

Scarlet Trumpet Honeysuckle 'Dropmore Scarlet'

Western Virgin's Bower
Clematis ligusticifolia

A vigorous native clematis that climbs readily with support. Do not cut back in fall. Produces clustered, white flowers summer to fall. Prefers fertile, well-drained soil. Height: 5–6m; width: 2–3m. Sun to P.M. sun.

Oxalis 'Sunset Velvet'

Boston Fern

Begonia 'Non-Stop Apricot'

Entrances

2
Getting
There

...the journey can be
as important as the destination...

For some people, sidewalks and driveways are strictly functional, designed to get the homeowner where he or she wants to go in the least amount of time with the fewest obstructions. These structures are often very linear, hard-edged and businesslike. Not many of us want a yard that looks like something out of Fritz Lang's *Metropolis*, so we introduce a border of bedding plants or shrubbery to soften the harsh, formal lines.

On the other hand, some people see a sidewalk as an opportunity to meander a bit, since the journey can be as important as the destination. People of this philosophical bent may choose stepping stones interspersed with groundcover perennials—often using varieties that offer not only visual appeal, but fragrance and texture, too. I've also seen winding paths of stepping stones broken up by low-growing species tulips, giving visitors the illusion of walking through an alpine meadow and not on a sidewalk at all. The beauty of the living sidewalk is that the sidewalk becomes part of the garden, rather than forming a cold, sterile border.

Of course, both approaches have their merits. Some people simply don't want to fuss with a perfectly functional sidewalk, while others can't bear to ignore the possibilities for experimentation. In my own yard, both worlds are represented. I have a clear driveway that serves a strictly functional purpose: it's where I park my car. But I also have a meandering slate path that leads to my back door.

The path you choose depends on your temperament. Will the engineer or the poet beat a path to your door? ✂

The solution to long, straight, boring sidewalks is to draw the eye from side to side with the strategic placement of asymmetrical flowerbeds, containers or feature plants.

We live in a neighbourhood where each home is fronted by a long expanse of boring lawn with long concrete sidewalks leading to the front door. We want our sunny front yard to be different, breaking up the distance between the street and our front entrance without ripping up the sidewalk. What grows here?

THERE ARE A FEW very simple and effective ways to deal with long expanses and each involves a little visual trickery. Plot a curving bed that bisects the walkway, perhaps in a gentle 'S' shape. This provides space for points of interest on both sides of the walk and serves to break up the length by drawing the eye from side to side, rather than directly ahead. Use a variety of plants of varying height and spread to divert the eye up- and downward. Finally, visually shorten the distance to your door by using plants that bloom in 'hot' colours, such as orange, red and yellow.

ANNUALS

Geranium 'Designer Bright Lilac'

A zonal geranium that is an ideal accent and excellent in containers and flowerbeds. Bright lilac with a lighter soft centre, extra large, double flowers. Height: 30–35cm. Sun to P.M. sun.

Poppy 'Orange King'

Beautiful, bright orange, 7cm, single flowers are lovely in mass displays. Grey, fine, thread-like foliage. Heat and drought tolerant. Height: 30cm; spacing: 25–30cm. Sun.

Rudbeckia 'Prairie Sun'

An award-winning variety prized for its 12cm, golden blooms, tipped in primrose yellow with light green centres. Height: 90cm. Sun.

Petunia, Madness Series

This series produces masses of solid or veined flowers available in many colours. Excellent in containers and flowerbeds. Single, 8cm flowers show superior weather tolerance. Heat and drought tolerant. Height: 25–30cm; spacing: 15–20cm. Sun to P.M. sun.

Petunia 'Madness Red'

Rudbeckia 'Prairie Sun'

Marigold 'Antigua Orange'

Geranium 'Designer Bright Lilac'

Paths

Daylily 'Chicago Fire'

Columbine 'Songbird Cardinal'

PERENNIALS

Daylily
Hemerocallis 'Chicago Fire'

Ideal for any mixed border. Eye-catching fire-engine red flowers appear in July. Divide every 3–5 years to maintain vigour. Prefers moist, fertile, well-drained soil. Height: 85cm; width: 45–90cm. Sun to P.M. sun.

False Sunflower
Heliopsis 'Loraine Sunshine'

Green and white variegated foliage makes this a great contrast plant suitable for any mixed border. Golden-yellow flowers bloom mid summer to fall and make excellent cutflowers. Clump-forming habit. Prefers fertile, well-drained, moist, organic soil but is quite heat and drought tolerant. Height: 60–90cm; width: 30–45cm. Sun to P.M. sun.

Columbine
Aquilegia 'Songbird Cardinal'

These striking crimson-red and white flowers bloom in spring on clump-forming plant. Prefers fertile, well-drained, moist soil. Height: 45–60cm; width: 45–60cm. Sun to P.M. sun.

False Sunflower 'Loraine Sunshine'

Roses

'George Vancouver' Explorer
Shrub

A lovely, lightly fragrant rose that is reliably hardy to Zone 3. Blooms present in clusters followed by hundreds of red rosehips in fall. Good resistance to mildew and blackspot. Produces semi-double, medium red, 6cm flowers June through summer. Height: 60–75cm; spread: 60–75cm. Sun.

Trees & Shrubs

Pine 'White Bud'
Pinus mugo

A low maintenance, naturally dwarf evergreen that sports bright white candles in spring. Useful in rock gardens and in mixed borders. Height: 1m; width: 1.5m. Sun to P.M. sun.

Spruce 'Dwarf Serbian'
Picea omorika 'Nana'

Beautiful, blue and dark green, bi-coloured foliage on a form that varies from globe-shaped to broadly pyramidal. Height: 3m; width: 2–3m in 50 years. Sun.

Rose 'George Vancouver'

Spruce 'Dwarf Serbian'

Pine 'White Bud'

Woolly thyme thrives between stepping stones providing colour, texture and scent.

We have a new flagstone path winding across our sunny yard and we'd like to plant in between and around the stones. What grows here?

THERE ARE MANY low-spreading perennials that will grow to fill in the spaces between flat stone slabs. When selecting plants, consider the amount of heat the flagstone path will absorb and the amount of foot traffic it will bear. Alpine plants often do well in these locations. For additional foliage, line the edges of the path with short shrubs and annuals.

ANNUALS

Nierembergia 'Purple Robe'
Ideal in mass displays or as an annual groundcover. Purple and white star-like, cup-shaped flowers on a plant with a neat compact habit. Height: 10–15cm; spacing: 10–15cm. Sun to P.M. sun.

PERENNIALS

Moss Campion
Silene acaulis
Forms a carefree evergreen, mossy mat topped with pink flowers in late spring to summer. Thrives in gritty, sharply-drained soil. Height: 2–5cm; width: 20–40cm. Sun to P.M. sun.

Turkish Speedwell
Veronica thymoides

Used in rock gardens and rocky slopes, this plant forms a dense mat. Deep blue to purple-blue flowers bloom in early summer atop grey-green foliage. Requires gritty, sharply-drained, organic soil—avoid winter wet. Height: 2cm; width 10–20cm. Sun to P.M. Sun.

Woolly Thyme
Thymus pseudolanuginosus

Thick, woolly, grey-green foliage forms a dense mat. Tolerates poor, dry sites once established. Plant between paving stones as it can withstand light foot traffic. Produces deep pink flowers in late spring to early summer. Thrives in well-drained, neutral to alkaline soil. Height: 1–2cm; width: 30–45+cm. Sun to P.M. sun.

ROSES

'Showy Pavement'
Pavement *Hybrid Rugosa*

A very hardy and attractive shrub rose with striking pink, 8-9cm flowers that bloom repeatedly. Lightly fragrant. Height: 60cm; spread: 90–100cm. Sun.

TREES & SHRUBS

Juniper 'Daub's Frosted'
Juniperus chinensis

A great accent groundcover with light golden-yellow new growth standing out against soft bluish-green older foliage. Pretty lining the edge of a path. Height: 30–40cm; width: 1.5m in 10 years. Sun.

Nierembergia 'Purple Robe'

Juniper 'Daub's Frosted'

Moss Campion

Rose 'Showy Pavement'

Bunchberry, with its creamy blooms and red berries, is an attractive groundcover for shady spots.

I have round stepping stones that run alongside my house and lead to a patio. Moss grows freely on the stones and the surrounding ground. I would like to incorporate other plants that will do well in this moist, shady area. What grows here?

MOIST, SHADY AREAS are a great spot for growing a variety of plants that range in height. Use shorter plants around and between the stones and place others, graduating in height, on the outer sides of the path.

ANNUALS

Mimulus, Mystic Series
Attractive in mass displays, borders and hanging baskets. This unique plant can grow almost anywhere. 5cm, open snapdragon-like flowers available in a range of colours. Height: 20–25cm; spacing: 15–20cm. Sun or shade.

PERENNIALS

Bunchberry
Cornus canadensis
This evergreen groundcover is good for naturalizing a shady area. Cream flow-
ers in early summer are followed by bright red, edible berries in fall. Prefers moist, acidic soil. Height: 10–20cm; width: 30+cm. Shade to A.M. sun.

Creeping Myrtle
Vinca minor
A great evergreen groundcover for a shady border or woodland garden. Dark green mat-forming foliage. Produces blue flowers from late spring to fall. Tolerates most types of soil. Prefers moist soils—avoid dry sites. Height: 10–20cm; width: 60+cm. Sun or shade.

Russian Cypress

Stemless Gentian

Heartleaf Bergenia
Bergenia cordifolia

A very versatile plant that grows in a wide range of soils and moisture conditions. Clump-forming, evergreen foliage spreads more rapidly in moist soils. Do not cut back in fall. Pale to dark pink flowers bloom in spring. Height: 40–45cm; width: 60cm. Sun or shade.

Stemless Gentian
Gentiana acaulis

Attractive along a path, abundant and large, blue flowers bloom spring to summer. Provides striking fall colour. Thrives in organic, moist, well-drained soil. Height: 10–15cm; width: 20–30cm. Shade to A.M. sun.

Heartleaf Bergenia

TREES & SHRUBS

Russian Cypress
Microbiota decussata

This is a great evergreen groundcover that spreads indefinitely. We know of a 14-year-old shrub that was 4m wide. Bright green foliage turns purple-brown in winter. Requires moist soil to look its best. Height: 30cm; width: 3–4m. Shade to A.M. sun.

Mimulus 'Mystic Yellow'

Use plants with strong forms like 'Coronation Triumph' potentilla to create interest in gravelled areas.

I have a sunny, hot side yard that has been covered in gravel. It looks very stark and barren. I'd like to soften the edges by incorporating plants that will outline a footpath and grow through the gravel. What grows here?

To create the contemporary, minimalist (and increasingly popular) look you are describing, select plants that do well in rock or alpine gardens and stay away from floppy, open forms. You do not need to fill in the entire area to make a statement. Instead, group pockets of plants together using a combination of textures and heights.

ANNUALS

Salvia 'Strata'
Salvia farinacea

An award-winning variety with narrow spikes of silvery-white and medium blue florets, similar to lavender. Attracts hummingbirds and makes a good cut or dried flower. Height: 30–35cm. Sun.

Wheat Celosia 'Flamingo Feather'
Celosia spicata

Heat and drought-tolerant celosia is superb planted in groups. Two-toned, silvery-pink and rose, 6–8cm, wheat-like flowers are often used for cut or dried flower arrangements. Height: 45–65cm; spacing: 25–35cm. Sun.

PERENNIALS

Blue Fescue
Festuca glauca

A wonderful drought-tolerant accent grass. Clump-forming, blue-green foliage with matching seed heads in summer. Considered evergreen. Snip blades to accent bouquets. Requires well-drained, dry soil. Height: 25–40cm; width: 25–30cm. Sun to P.M. sun.

Cushion Spurge
Euphorbia polychroma

This spurge forms a neat mound and never spreads from its allotted space. Bright chartreuse-yellow bracts appear in spring. Tolerant of poor soils, it prefers well-drained, sandy soils and a hot and dry location. Height: 40–60cm; width: 40–60cm. Sun.

Blue Fescue

Salvia 'Strata'

Wheat Celosia 'Flamingo Feather'

Soapwell

Showy Stonecrop 'Autumn Joy'

Cushion Spurge

Showy Stonecrop
Sedum 'Autumn Joy'

Striking planted in scree or gravel, this *sedum* has a clump-forming, upright habit. Clustered, deep pink flowers fading to copper-red appear in late summer to fall. Although tolerant of poor soils and dry periods it prefers well-drained, moderately fertile soil. Height: 45–60cm; width: 45–60cm. Sun to P.M. sun.

Soapwell
Yucca glauca

Valued for their bold upright form, yuccas grow best in a sheltered site away from cold, drying winds. Sword-like, evergreen foliage highlighted by waxy, white flowers in late summer. Do not cut back. Requires well-drained soil—avoid winter wet. Height: 30–70cm; width: 60cm. Sun.

Thyme Leaf Speedwell
Veronica oltensis

Thrives in rock gardens or on rocky slopes. Mat-forming foliage and sub-shrubby habit supports azure-blue flowers from late spring to summer. Requires gritty, sharply-drained, organic, alkaline soil. Height: 5–8cm; width: 15–20cm. Sun to P.M. sun.

Roses

'Therese Bugnet'
Hybrid Rugosa

Hardy to Zone 1 and flowering on
old wood, this intensely fragrant rose
blooms from mid June, repeating until
frost. 8–10cm flowers are double and
medium pink in colour. Height: 2m;
spread: 1.5m. Sun.

Trees & Shrubs

Pine 'Morel Red'
Pinus resinosa

Long, soft-to-touch needles on a compact, maturing to dense, informal form.
Great for large shrub beds. Height: 2m;
width: 1.5–2m. Sun.

Potentilla 'Coronation Triumph'
Potentilla fruticosa

Great for hedging, borders or as a feature in shrub beds. One of the largest
cultivars available. Abundant yellow
blooms in summer. Thrives in a hot,
dry site. Height: 1m; width: 1m. Sun.

Rose 'Therese Bugnet'

Potentilla 'Coronation Triumph'

Pine 'Morel Red'

Thyme Leaf Speedwell

Annuals like 'Bonanza Flame' marigolds provide colour all summer beside your driveway and make it easier to deal with snow in the winter.

I have a long driveway running alongside my front yard and would like to place a flowerbed against it. Snow is piled here each winter. What grows here?

SINCE SNOW IS stored here, you have several factors to consider: the weight of the snow, salt content and the fact that it may be one of the last areas to thaw in spring. When you have children, the possibility of trampling or digging in the snow bank adds another concern. If you want to use perennials or shrubs, choose very resilient plants and when you pile snow on the bed, place it around the plants first, not directly on top to avoid breaking branches. Another concern is slope—most driveways slant downward to the street, creating a run-off situation for any beds sloping in the same direction. Apply mulch, whether it is gravel or shredded bark, to slow run-off and preserve the soil.

ANNUALS

Dianthus, Floral Lace Series

Very attractive grown en masse in borders and garden beds. Large 4cm, lacy-fringed flowers available in solid colours, bicolours or as a mix. Compact, bushy growth habit. Quite frost tolerant. Height: 20–25cm; spacing: 15–20cm. Sun.

Marigold, Bonanza Series

A heat tolerant plant excellent in mass displays, containers and borders. Available in a wide range of colours. Large 5cm, double flowers. Height: 20cm; spacing: 15–20cm. Sun to P.M. sun.

Snapdragon, Floral Showers Series

A very short traditional snapdragon producing bushy and full, early-flowering plants with excellent garden performance—great in mass plantings and for borders. Available in a wide range of colours. Quite frost tolerant. Height: 15–20cm; width 20–25cm. Sun.

PERENNIALS

Blue Sage
Salvia nemorosa 'East Friesland'

Clump forming with a compact habit, this plant is suitable for a mixed border. Violet-blue flowers in summer are good as a cut flower. Cut back after blooming for second flush of flowers. Thrives in well-drained, moist, organic soil. Height: 45–60cm; width: 45–60cm. Sun to P.M. sun.

Bouncing Bet
Saponaria officinalis 'Rosea Plena'

An upright form suitable for a mixed border. Fragrant, double, rose-pink flowers bloom summer to fall. Although drought tolerant, it prefers well-drained, fertile soil. Height: 60–90cm; width: 60–90cm. Sun to P.M. sun.

Snapdragon 'Floral Showers Yellow'

Blue Sage 'East Friesland'

Dianthus 'Floral Lace Cherry'

Bouncing Bet

Old Man Sage

Daylily 'Holiday Delight'

Daylily
Hemerocallis 'Holiday Delight'

A resilient plant for a border. Orange flowers with a red eye bloom in July. Divide every 3–5 years to maintain vigour. Thrives in moist, fertile, well-drained soil. Height: 70cm; width: 45–75cm. Sun to P.M. sun.

Old Man Sage
Artemisia abrotanum

Grown strictly for its feathery, green, aromatic foliage which is used as an accent. This upright form is dense and shrub like. Reputed to repel ants and aphids. Prune back hard in spring. Thrives in well-drained, alkaline, poor, dry soils in a hot location. Height: 90–100cm; width: 90–100cm. Sun.

Sea Thrift
Armeria maritima 'Dusseldorf Pride'

In spring, ball-like, deep pink blooms are held atop grass-like, clump-forming foliage—perfect for rock gardens or the front of borders. Deadhead regularly to prolong blooming but do not cut foliage back. Will tolerate poor soils, but prefers them to be well-drained. Height: 15–20cm; width: 30cm. Sun to P.M. sun.

Sea Thrift 'Dusseldorf Pride'

ROSES

'Dwarf Pavement' Pavement
Hybrid Rugosa

Pavement roses may be the most salt-tolerant roses ever developed. They have a low, sprawling growth habit and make a hardy, attractive groundcover or feature shrub. Semi-double, dark pink, 6–8cm flowers with a mild fragrance bloom repeatedly through summer. Height: 75–90cm; spread: 90cm. Sun.

TREES & SHRUBS

Pine 'Slowmound'
Pinus mugo

Dark green needles and upright spring candles on a very slow-growing pine. A great dwarf plant for confined sites. Does not require pruning to maintain shape. Height: 60–75cm; width: 1–1.5m in 15 years. Sun.

Rose 'Dwarf Pavement'

Pine 'Slowmound'

Driveways

Feature plants like the gigantic 'Big Leaf' elephant ears will add appeal to any driveway.

Our garage front faces the street and is quite boring to look at. We'd like to use some plants to add curb appeal, but the paved driveway runs right up to the building. What grows here?

ADD THE CHARM you are looking for by using large containers of colourful plants. Often, when people place pots or urns in these locations they make the mistake of using ones that are too small. The result is that they look out of proportion, don't provide visual impact and they often blow over or dry out too quickly. To add height, use an obelisk in the pot or mount sturdy brackets onto the garage and fill large hanging baskets with colourful, trailing plants.

ANNUALS

Calibrachoa 'Million Bells Terracotta'

A fast-growing, heavy-blooming and self-cleaning plant that thrives in hanging baskets, containers, or grown as an annual groundcover. 'Terracotta' has small, petunia-like, deep orange-throated, peach-bronze blooms. Height: 8–15cm; trails to 60cm. Sun.

Elephant Ears 'Big Leaf'

Colocasia

An interesting bulb that makes an excellent feature plant, producing large, elephant ear-like, exotic foliage. Protect from hot sun and wind. Height: up to 2m. Shade to A.M. sun.

Pennisetum 'Fountain Grass'

Adds a nice dimension to beds and containers. Ornamental grassy foliage arches and waves in the wind. Produces rosy-hued seed heads. Height: 60–90cm; spacing: 45–75cm. Sun to P.M. sun.

Rudbeckia 'Autumn Colours'

Superb in mass displays, borders and containers. Vivid red rings on golden, 12cm, daisy-like flowers with brown centres. Excellent cutflower. Height: 50cm; spacing: 30cm. Sun.

Rudbeckia 'Autumn Colours'

Calibrachoa 'Million Bells Terracotta'

Pennisetum 'Fountain Grass'

Sweet Potato Vine 'Marguerite'

Scaevola 'Blue Ribbon'

This Australian native is also known as Australian Fan Flower. It is striking in hanging baskets and mixed planters. Heat and drought-tolerant, producing small, lavender, fan-shaped flowers along upright-bending stems. Height: 20–25cm; spreads to 30cm. Sun to P.M. sun.

Sweet Potato Vine 'Marguerite'

A lush, fast-growing vine covered with large, lime green, heart-shaped leaves. Best used in containers or baskets but can be grown as a groundcover. Height: 10–15cm; trails to 75cm. Sun to P.M. sun.

Strobilanthes 'Persian Shield'

An ideal moisture-loving contrast plant. Striking, iridescent foliage with a well-branched habit. Height: up to 60cm; spacing: 30cm. Shade to A.M. sun.

Scaevola 'Blue Ribbon'

Verbena 'Aztec Lavender'

Rose 'Starry Night'

Verbena 'Aztec Lavender'

Outstanding performance in hanging baskets, mixed planters and garden beds displaying large, bright rosy-lavender, clustered flowers; has a mounding and trailing growth habit. Height: up to 20cm; trails to 50cm. Sun.

ROSES

'Ingrid Bergman' *Hybrid Tea*

A vigorous, compact tender rose, excellent for a hot site. Double, bright red, 10–15cm flowers bloom June through summer. Light rose fragrance. Height: 60–75cm; spread: 75cm. Sun.

'Starry Night' *Tender Shrub*

Great for training on an obelisk or trellis. Large clusters of single bright white, 4–6cm flowers bloom from June and continuously through summer. Light fragrance. Height: 60–75cm; spread: 100–150cm. Sun.

Rose 'Ingrid Bergman'

Snow on the mountain, a rapid-spreading and aggressive groundcover, is an excellent choice in contained areas.

I have a long, weedy strip of poor soil behind my garage, facing the back alley. I would like an inexpensive and simple way to make this area more attractive. What grows here?

THERE ARE LOTS OF PLANTS that will spread quickly to cover a long area, require minimal attention and be tolerant of less than desirable soil conditions. Some will self-seed annually, root where they touch soil or spread underground. If the area is well contained by a building, paved driveway or sidewalk, aggressive plants can be used without fear of them taking over your yard.

ANNUALS

Calendula 'Pacific Beauty Mix'
This no fuss annual produces double, peach, orange, gold and yellow flowers and has a uniform growth habit—ideal in tall borders. Makes an excellent cutflower. Height: 40–45cm; spacing: 20–25cm. Sun to P.M. sun.

PERENNIALS

Lily-of-the-Valley
Convallaria majalis
A vigorous, spreading and dense groundcover for moist or dry areas. Tiny, pendant, bell-shaped, white flowers appear in spring and are fragrant. Attractive orange-red berries follow in fall. Prefers organic, well-drained, moist soil but is tolerant of dry sites. Height: 15–20cm; width: 45–60+cm. Sun or shade.

Cypress Spurge

Euphorbia cyparissias 'Fens Ruby'

Use in a wild garden where it will contrast nicely and spread without troubling other plants. Produces feathery, blue-green foliage and yellow bracts that age to purplish-red in spring. Prefers well-drained, dry, sandy soil. Height: 20–40cm; width: 30–40+cm. Sun.

Maltese Cross

Lychnis chalcedonica

Grow in a cottage garden or mixed border where it can self-seed freely. Cross-shaped, scarlet-red flowers in early summer to mid summer provide a splash of brilliant red colour that attracts hummingbirds. Upright, stiff stems may need support. Prefers moist, fertile soil. Height: 90–120cm; width: 20–30cm. Sun to P.M. sun.

Mullein

Verbascum 'Summer Sorbet'

A long-blooming but short-lived perennial that makes a wonderful addition to a border. Clump-forming foliage supports raspberry-peach flowers in mid summer and attracts hummingbirds. Prefers sandy, alkaline, well-drained, poor soil. Height: 45–60cm; width: 30–45cm. Sun.

Snow on the Mountain

Aegopodium podagraria 'Variegatum'

A rapid and aggressive, spreading groundcover that needs to be contained. Green and white variegated foliage produces dainty white flowers that resemble those on Queen Anne's Lace. Tolerates poor soil but not drought. Height: 30–60cm; width: 60+cm. Sun or shade.

Calendula 'Pacific Beauty Orange'

Cypress Spurge 'Fens Ruby'

Maltese Cross

Mullein 'Summer Sorbet'

'Vintage Mix' stocks are a great choice for borders because of their fragrance and attractive flower spikes.

Our patio is surrounded on two sides by newly dug beds. We'd like to have a variety of fragrant plants in this sunny area. What grows here?

GROWING FRAGRANT plants where you can sit and enjoy them is one of the pleasures and rewards of planning your garden well. Choose plants with some thought to having a continuously fragrant bed, not one that blooms all at once. You may also want to consider how the scents of different plants vary throughout the day.

ANNUALS

Stocks, Vintage Series

Stocks are an old-fashioned favourite prized for their fragrance and pretty blooms. This series produces double-flowering spikes on compact, bushy plants that bloom early. Available in beautiful individual or mixed shades. Performs well in flowerbeds and containers. Height: 30 cm; spacing: 20cm. Sun.

Heliotrope 'Marine Blue'

These strongly fragrant flowers attract hummingbirds. Large, 25cm, clustered blooms are deep purple—a lovely addition to pots and patio beds. Height: 35cm; spacing: 25–30cm. Sun.

PERENNIALS

Alpine Pink
Dianthus microlepis

This cushion-forming plant produces pink to purple flowers in summer, with a carnation-like scent. Foliage is blue-grey and evergreen—do not cut back. Prefers sharply-drained, acidic soil—avoid winter wet. Height: 5–10 cm; width: 10–20cm. Sun to P.M. sun.

Catmint
Nepeta racemosa

Nepeta's mint-scented foliage has a spreading, upright habit. Brightens up any mixed border with spiked, violet-blue flowers summer to fall and is long blooming and drought tolerant. Trim after flowering to keep compact. Prefers well-drained soil. Height: 30cm; width: 30–45cm. Sun to P.M. sun.

ROSES

'Blanc Double De Coubert'
Hybrid Rugosa

A hardy shrub rose with strongly fragrant blooms that fade and darken with age. Hardy to Zone 1—great for hedges. Semi-double, white, 6–8cm flowers bloom June to September. Height: 1.5m; spread: 1.5m. Sun.

TREES & SHRUBS

Mockorange 'Blizzard'
Philadelphus lewisii

Abundant orange-scented, white blooms appear in June on this very hardy accent or background shrub. Foliage turns yellow-orange in fall. Prune immediately after blooming is finished. Height: 1–1.5m; width: 1–1.5m. Sun to P.M. sun.

Patios & Decks

Heliotrope 'Marine Blue'

Mockorange 'Blizzard'

Alpine Pink

Catmint

Russian olive not only thrives in hot sunny areas, it is also easily pruned to a needed form, making it ideal for use near decks and patios.

I want to plant some small trees around my sunny, hot deck and its adjoining ground-level patio. I don't want anything with messy fruit. What grows here?

THERE ARE A NUMBER of tidy trees that don't drop fruit and seeds and are available in a variety of shapes. Columnar, open-headed and teardrop forms, for example, will provide you with shade and, when used in combination, a very interesting landscape. Use smaller trees around the ground-level patio and taller ones at the sides of the raised deck.

Patios & Decks

Trees & Shrubs

Amur Maackia
Maackia amurensis
Perfect for small yards and very showy. This globe-shaped tree's foliage is fine textured with golden bark. Creamy-white, fragrant blooms appear in mid summer. Plant in a sheltered site. Height: 6–10m; width: 6–7m. Sun.

Flowering Plum 'Princess Kay'
Prunus nigra
A great feature tree for small yards. Considered a heavy bloomer with showy white, fragrant, double blooms in spring. Its purplish-black bark is attractive in winter. Height: 3–5m; width: 2–3m. Sun.

Flowering Plum 'Muckle'
Prunus x *nigrella*
A slow-growing and extremely hardy tree that makes a great focal point for small yards. In early spring showy rosy-pink blooms cover this tiny tree. Produces no fruit. Height: 3–4m; width: 3–3.5m. Sun.

Lilac 'Madame Lemoine'
Syringa vulgaris
Keep this large shrub pruned to 3–5 stems for best display and form. Lovely white, fragrant, double blooms appear in mid spring. Spreading habit. Height: 2–3m; width: 2–3m. Sun to P.M. sun.

Pear 'Mountain Frost'
Pyrus ussuriensis 'Bailfrost'
A showy ornamental tree with an upright growth habit. Pretty white blooms in May followed by very sparse 2cm fruit. Nice yellow fall colour. Height: 7–8m; width: 5–6m. Sun.

Russian Olive
Elaegnus angustifolia
A round-headed tree that is also sold in shrub form. Silvery leaves and dark bark contrast well with evergreen backgrounds. Very fragrant, tiny, yellow blooms appear in June. Thrives in a hot, dry site. Height: 6–10m; width: 6–10m. Sun.

Flowering Plum 'Muckle'

Lilac 'Madame Lemoine'

Amur Maackia

3

Nasty Necessities

…a little patience and planning…

Everyone seems to have at least one spot in the yard that's a bit of an eyesore. It could be an awkwardly placed utility pole or power box, a stand of garbage cans or the compost pile. You can ignore these aggravations for a while, but eventually, they begin to scream for some kind of beautification. When you're faced with a problem of this nature, sweeping it under the carpet—metaphorically, of course—may be just the thing.

The barrier between my yard and the severe slope of the adjacent ravine is a rather industrial-looking, galvanized chain link fence supported by angle iron stakes and steel posts at each end. For safety's sake it is a necessary evil, but frankly, it's hideous.

The choice was either to rip it down and erect something more pleasing to my eye or to work with what I had. I chose to use the chain link and add some modifications. I ran a bed of enriched soil about 60 cm wide along its base and installed a strip of landscape edging to separate the bed from my lawn. At intervals, I planted several varieties of clematis. I laid bark mulch around the base of each plant to keep the weeds in check and the roots cool and moist. Finally, I painted the end posts black to make them fade into the background.

Within a couple of years, the clematis vines had woven their way through the chain links and intermingled with one another, completely covering the barrier and providing spectacular flowers during the spring and summer. Even during the winter, the fence is barely visible, because the dormant vines block out the repetitious chain-link pattern.

With a little work, I transformed an ugly but necessary feature of my yard into a dynamic, living wall of colour. With a little patience and planning, you can do the same. So don't feel bad about sweeping a problem under the carpet—especially if it's a carpet of flowers. ❧

Camouflaging utility devices is a challenge but not impossible with a little planning.

On the edge of our property there is a streetlight mounted on an ugly, grey power box. We would like to disguise as much of it as possible. What grows here?

WHEN DEALING WITH any type of utility device, you must consider access for repairs and maintenance. First, contact the utility company to find out what the regulations are concerning planting and use of the area and arrange to have the underground cables marked. Dig a bed out from the base of the box (at the required distance), large enough to accommodate full, dense plants that will provide coverage throughout as much of the year as possible. You can choose a single plant, but using plants with varying heights will create a more appealing and year-round camouflage.

ANNUALS

Cactus Dahlia 'Park Princess'
Dahlias are great in patio pots and in flowerbeds. This bulb is lifted in fall to overwinter. Large, starburst-type flowers are deep rose with light tips—superb cutflowers. Height: up to 60cm. Sun to P.M. sun.

Marigold 'Jubilee Mix'
Excellent in backgrounds or grown as an annual hedge. Lemon, golden-yellow and orange, 8cm, fully double flowers are supported by strong sturdy stems. Height: 75–80cm; spacing: 30–35cm. Sun.

Snapdragon, Rocket Series

This is a traditional tall snapdragon available in individual colours or a mix. Ideal in backgrounds with extra long spikes of blooms that are excellent as cutflowers. Height: 75–90cm; spacing: 30cm. Sun.

PERENNIALS

Knautia

Knautia macedonica

A very interesting clump-forming perennial with small, pincushion-like, dark purple to red flowers in summer. Suitable for a cottage or natural garden. Prefers well-drained, moderately fertile, alkaline soil. Height: 60–80cm; width: 30–45cm. Sun to P.M. sun.

Monkshood

Aconitum napellus

A strongly upright perennial prized for its indigo-blue flowers in late summer. Prefers moist, fertile, cool soil and tolerates partial shade. Height: 90–150cm; width: 30–60cm. Sun to P.M. sun.

Dahlia 'Park Princess'

Knautia

Snapdragon 'Rocket Red'

Monkshood

Peony
Paeonia 'Peppermint'

Peonies are slow growing but long-lived perennials that benefit from the extra support of a wire hoop. Plant eyes 5cm deep. Double, pale pink flowers with red flecks bloom in spring. Thrives in moist, acid-free, fertile, well-drained soil. Height: 90cm; width: 90–100cm. Sun to P.M. sun.

Peony
Paeonia 'Henry Bockstoce'

This variety is generally more compact, blooms earlier and has thicker stems that hold up better to adverse weather conditions. Deep red flowers in spring atop clump-forming foliage. Plant eyes 5cm deep. Thrives in moist, acid-free, fertile, well-drained soil. Height: 75cm; width: 60–90cm. Sun to P.M. sun.

ROSES

'Hansa'
Hybrid Rugosa

One of the best all-round rugosas—very long-lived, dense in form and hardy to Zone 1. Double, fuchsia-red, 8–10cm flowers have a strong clove-like fragrance. Blooms in June or July and repeats all summer. Height: 1.5–2m; spread: 1.5–2m. Sun.

TREES & SHRUBS

Chokeberry 'Autumn Magic'
Aronia melonocarpa

A really lovely shrub with fragrant, clustered white blooms in spring followed by clusters of purple fruit. Striking red and orange fall colours. Height: 1.5–2m; width: 1.5–2m. Sun.

Rose 'Hansa'

Chokeberry 'Autumn Magic'

Peony 'Henry Bockstoce'

Cotoneaster 'Hedge'
Cotoneaster acutifolius

Also known as 'Peking.' A very hardy
and useful shrub, traditionally sheared
and shaped for formal hedging but
is equally attractive left to arch in its
natural form. Plant 30–45cm apart
for hedges. Dark green, dense foliage
turns a lovely orange-red colour in fall.
Height: 2–3m; width: 2–3m. Sun to
P.M. sun.

Juniper 'Savin'
Juniperus sabina

A distinct vase-shaped, dense form that
is great in large shrub beds. Very dark
green foliage turns much paler in winter. Height: 1.5m; width: 1.5–3m. Sun.

Spiraea 'Goldmound'
Spiraea japonica

A mound of iridescent yellow-gold foliage that makes a colourful accent and
border plant. Pinkish blooms appear
in summer. Height: 90–100cm; width:
90–100cm. Sun to P.M. sun.

Willow 'Dwarf Arctic Blue Leaf'
Salix purpurea 'Nana'

Very attractive, deep blue foliage on a
dense, compact form with light grey
bark. Provides great contrast in shrub
beds. Try it as an informal hedge. Prefers moist soil. Height: 1–1.5m; width:
1–1.5m. Sun.

Cotoneaster 'Hedge'

Willow 'Dwarf Arctic Blue Leaf'

Juniper 'Savin'

A free-standing trellis and an attractive vine like Virginia creeper can help screen an eyesore.

Our garbage cans are stored at the side of our home and are visible from the street. We would like to disguise them with plants, but not reduce access. This area is shady in the morning. What grows here?

I F THE AREA IN FRONT of the receptacles is not paved, erect a single lattice trellis in front of the cans. Grow plants on it, plant in front of it or, alternatively, mount a hanging basket on it. This will provide instant and all-season coverage and allow you to choose from a variety of plants. If the area is paved, place a large planter with a fan trellis or obelisk covered in climbing annual vines to provide seasonal disguise.

ANNUALS

Nasturtium 'Forest Flame'
An heirloom variety, with a very vigorous trailing habit and a profusion of blooms. Use in hanging baskets or spilling out of containers. Golden apricot-orange, double flowers with striking variegated foliage. Trails: 60–90cm; spacing: 25–30cm. Sun.

PERENNIALS

Alpine Clematis
Clematis alpina 'Pink Flamingo'

Produces a lush, pest-free screen early in spring. Grow as a very hardy climber with support, groundcover or trailing over stone walls. Pretty semi-double, nodding, pink flowers in spring. Requires fertile, well-drained soil and cool roots. Do not cut back. Height: 2–3m; width: 2m. Sun to P.M. sun.

Chinese Rhubarb
Rheum palmatum 'Atrosanguineum'

This big, tropical-looking plant has leaves that can be up to 90cm across. Best with at least full A.M. sun to deepen the foliage colour. Tolerates full sun if planted in cool, moist soil. Clump-forming; lobed, palmate foliage is crimson-red when young producing crimson-red flower spikes in early summer. Deep, moist, organic soil. Height: 2–2.5m; width: 1.2–1.8m. Sun or shade.

Virginia Creeper
Parthenocissus quinquefolia

This vine will easily cover a fence, wall or tree stump. Provide support for this vigorous climber. Ivy-like foliage turns brilliant red in fall. Green-white flowers appear in summer followed by blue-black fruit. Do not cut back in fall. Prefers fertile, well-drained soil. Height: 5–10m; width: 2–3+m. Sun or shade.

TREES & SHRUBS

Dogwood 'Isanti'
Cornus stolonifera

Useful for screens or borders, this shrub provides a showy accent in winter. A compact, green-leafed variety with bright red stems. Height: 1.5–2m; width: 1.5–2m. Sun to P.M. sun.

Maple 'Bailey Compact'
Acer tataricum ssp. *ginnala*

A compact variety—terrific for small yards and for screening. Foliage turns bright red in fall. Height: 2–3m; width: 2–3m. Sun to P.M. sun.

Alpine Clematis 'Pink Flamingo'

Maple 'Bailey Compact'

Chinese Rhubarb

Dogwood 'Isanti'

When choosing plants to screen areas, consider shrubs like 'Golden' elder that offer blooms, colour and form.

We have a large, noisy air conditioner in our backyard. We would like to make it less obvious in the landscape. The area is quite sunny. What grows here?

AIR CONDITIONING UNITS pull outside air in through their sides while expelling hot air through the top. Consequently, you must leave room for air circulation, as well as repairs, maintenance and possible removal and replacement. Any plants must be a kept at a minimum distance of 60cm from all sides of the unit. Avoid plants that produce fluffy seeds which can block the air conditioner's coils. Planting a dense, sound-blocking hedge is one way of screening. Quick growing annuals and tall perennials will also offer some camouflage, but only seasonally.

ANNUALS

Cleome 'Queen Mix'
A tall, old-fashioned favourite, ideally used in backgrounds. Large, 12–15cm, spider-like flowers are available in shades of rose, violet, cherry and white. Quite tolerant of heat and drought. Height: up to 100cm; spacing: 25–35cm. Sun.

Sunflower 'Ikarus'
A nicely branching sunflower. Produces many bright lemon-yellow, 10–15cm blooms that are excellent for cut flowers. Height: 1.2m; spacing: 45–60cm. Sun.

PERENNIALS

Daylily
Hemerolcalis 'Pardon Me'

A shorter daylily for the front border. Divide every 3–5 years to maintain vigour. Fragrant, bright red flowers bloom in July and may re-bloom in the fall. Prefers moist, fertile, well-drained soil. Height: 45cm; width: 30–60cm. Sun to P.M. sun.

Mugwort
Artemisia vulgaris 'Oriental Limelight'

A tough upright accent plant for difficult spots—extremely tolerant of hot and dry sites. Prune hard in spring. Dense, variegated, cream and green foliage. Prefers well-drained, alkaline, poor, dry soil. Height: 60–170cm; width: 30–100cm. Sun to P.M. sun.

TREES & SHRUBS

Barberry 'Emerald Carousel'
Berberis 'Tara'

A versatile plant. Yellow clustered blooms appear mid spring, followed by bright red berries. Deep green leaves turn reddish-purple in fall and woody, dense stems are attractive covered in snow. Use for hedging, small shrub beds and borders. Avoid wet soil. Height: 1–1.5m; width: 1–1.5m. Sun to P.M. sun.

Cedar 'Hetz Midget'
Thuja occidentalis

Dense foliage on a slow-growing, globe-shaped form make this a cedar for the rock garden, shrub bed or a formal hedge. Height: 90cm; width: 90cm. Sun to P.M. sun.

Elder 'Golden'
Sambucus racemosa 'Aurea'

Striking, bright yellow foliage provides contrast and makes a good screen. Attracts birds. Clustered white blooms appear in spring followed by red berries. Prefers moist soil. Height: 1.5–4m; width: 1.5–4m. Sun.

Cleome 'Queen Mix'

Sunflower 'Ikarus'

Daylily 'Pardon Me'

Utilities

Clarkia 'Mix' is a carefree, old-fashioned favourite that will easily hide the utility areas low on the walls of your home.

There is an unsightly gas meter mounted right next to my back door. I know I must leave it exposed, but I would like to make it less visible. What grows here?

YOU CAN PLANT in front of the meter, as long as the plants you choose grow no taller than the meter or can be pruned regularly to allow for visibility. This will disguise the pipe work and camouflage the meter itself somewhat. You can also custom design a trellis with a cut-out porthole, making sure to be diligent about training and pruning any climbing vines around the meter's face.

ANNUALS

Clarkia 'Mix'
Pretty in mass displays and undemanding. Large, rosette-like double flowers in pink, red, mauve, salmon and white make good cutflowers. Height: 60cm; spacing: 15–20cm. P.M. sun.

PERENNIALS

Bushy Aster
Aster x *dumosus* 'Jenny'
Double, red flowers bloom from late summer to fall on a clump-forming plant. Suitable for any mixed border, but avoid over crowding. Prefers moist, fertile, well-drained soil—water at base. Height: 45–75cm; width: 50–75cm. Sun to P.M. sun.

Fernleaf Yarrow
Achillea filipendulina
'Cloth of Gold'

A tall, upright plant with intense yellow flowers blooming continuously in summer. Thrives in a hot and dry location. Height: 45cm; width: 60–90cm. Sun to P.M. sun.

ROSES

'Henry Kelsey' Explorer
Hybrid Kordesii

This Explorer rose climbs or spreads to a wide bush. Produces large clusters of double, red, 6–8cm flowers with a spicy fragrance from July to frost. Hardy to Zone 2. Height: 2–3m; spread: 2–3m. Sun.

TREES & SHRUBS

Azalea 'Mandarin Lights'
Rhododendron

An excellent feature plant for small shrub beds. Flowerbuds are hardy to -35°C and open to masses of bright mandarin-orange blooms in late spring. Very hardy plant with upright, rounded form. Height: 1–1.5m; width: 1–1.5m. Sun to P.M. sun.

Willow 'Blue Fox'
Salix brachycarpa

Great for foundation plantings and shrub beds. Attractive blue-green foliage on a compact willow. Moist soil. Height: 1–1.5m; width: 1–1.5m. Sun to P.M. sun.

Willow 'Blue Fox'

Azalea 'Mandarin Lights'

Rose 'Henry Kelsey'

'Wichita Blue' juniper makes a great screen that will hide utilities from view, but be sure to consider its mature height and width.

Our water outlet and hose reel are located at the side of our house. The area under the tap is often soggy, even though it is covered by grass. We'd like to hide the tap and hose, but still have them easy to get to and use. What grows here?

A GREAT WAY TO DEAL with this utility area is to wall it in with plants, effectively making a contained room within the garden. Mark out the amount of space you need for the hose reel and any other tools you keep there, allowing for ample room to manoeuvre in and out of the area. Consider installing hose guides (pegs that direct the hose without damaging the plants). Replace the grass inside the area with paved stepping stones and proceed to create 'walls' along the outer edge. Create the walls with trellis and climbing vines or plant formal or informal, dense hedging material.

ANNUALS

Cosmos 'Seashells Mix'
Cosmos bipinnatus
Plant in a tight row to provide a low hedge effect. Pink, rose, cream and red, 10cm, trumpet-petaled flowers—good cutflower. Heat and drought tolerant. Height: 90cm; spacing: 30–40cm. Sun.

Utilities

PERENNIALS

Big Leaf Rayflower
Ligularia dentata 'Othello'
A hot, tropical look for the garden. Avoid windy sites. Purple foliage. Clump-forming, upright habit. Clustered, orange-yellow flowers in summer. Requires very moist, deep, moderately fertile soil. Height: 90–120cm; width: 60–90cm. Shade to A.M. sun.

Vine Bower
Clematis viticella 'Venosa Violacea'
Makes a hardy, lush, pest-free and easy-to-grow screen. It needs a support and cool roots. Produces stunning white flowers with purple veins in summer, followed by very attractive seed heads. Cut back in late fall. Thrives in fertile, well-drained soil. Height: 2–3m; width: 1–2m. Sun to P.M. sun.

ROSES

'Champlain' Explorer
Hybrid Kordesii
This rose is disease resistant and hardy to Zone 3. Double, dark red, 6–7cm flowers bloom continuously through summer and fall and produce a light fragrance. Height: 90cm; spread: 90cm. Sun.

Big Leaf Rayflower 'Othello'

TREES & SHRUBS

Juniper 'Wichita Blue'
Juniperus scopulorum
Brilliant silvery-blue foliage on a fast-growing, cone-shaped juniper. Can be made compact by shearing annually. Great for large shrub beds, rock gardens or screening. Height: 5–6m; width: 1.5–2m. Sun.

Lilac 'Tinkerbelle'
Syringa x 'Bailbelle'
Compact, upright growth—great for hedges, borders or as a feature shrub. A non-suckering variety. Rich wine buds open to deep pink, spicy-scented blooms in June. Height: 1.5–2m; width: 1.5m. Sun to P.M. sun.

Spiraea 'Crispa'
Spiraea japonica
Makes a lovely, low, informal hedge. Unique crinkled and twisted foliage is reddish-green, highlighting pink blooms in summer. Remove spent blooms for repeat flowering. Height: 60–90cm; width: 90–100cm. Sun.

Vine Bower 'Venosa Violacea'

Rose 'Champlain'

A thick stand of 'Custer' corn will disguise an unappealing composting unit, and the stalks can even be left standing over winter.

I have a bulky composter in a sunny corner of my vegetable garden. This composter is an essential part of my gardening practice, but it is not very attractive to look at. What grows here?

AS LONG AS YOU LEAVE the unit accessible, there is no reason not to make use of the nutrient-rich compost and plant around the composter. Erect a couple of tall and sturdy panels of chicken wire or plastic netting in front of the composter. Plant fast-growing vines and climbing vegetables that will thrive in the sun and soil in the area to effectively screen out your unsightly composter and, perhaps, provide you with a bumper crop.

FRUIT

Chokecherry 'Garrington'

Prunus

Pretty white blooms are followed by purplish-black, 8–10mm fruit in July and August. Use fruit for wine, jam or eat fresh. Cross-pollinates with most cherries. Height: 1.5–2m; width: 1.5m. Sun.

Raspberry 'Souris'

Rubus

A hardy raspberry with heavy fruit production. Red, sweet fruit is ready for harvest mid July to mid August. Enjoy fresh or preserved. Height: 1.5m width: 1m. Sun.

VEGETABLE

Corn 'Custer'

A few staggered rows of corn provide a pretty screen. This variety is sugar enhanced with tender, light gold kernels that have an excellent flavour. Grows 20cm cobs. Matures early August.

Cucumber 'Diva'

An award-winning variety with a vining habit and high yields. A superb self-pollinating salad cucumber with smooth, thin skin—no peeling required. Produces sweetly flavoured, semi-glossy, 15–20cm, slender, burpless and seedless cucumbers. Sun.

Pea 'Knight'

A vining pea that produces two pods per flower. Early season harvest. Vigorous growth habit. Height: up to 60cm. Sun.

Scarlet Runner Bean

A very ornamental and vigorous pole bean. The vines sport scarlet flowers followed by green, 15cm beans. Can grow up poles, trellises and fences. Late July to early August harvest. Height: 2+m. Sun.

Raspberry 'Souris'

Scarlet Runner Bean

Pea 'Knight'

'Walker' caragana can be trained to a narrow, graceful form that provides a visual break.

Our garage is attached to our house and we would like to visually separate them. What grows here?

IF YOU HAVE A PLANTING space in front of the connecting wall, use a plant with a tall, columnar form. If the area is paved, try a large container with tall plantings on a trellis or obelisk, or hang a basket with trailing blooms on the wall between the two buildings.

ANNUALS

Canna Lily Designer 'Orange Punch'
Great in containers and gardens. This bulb can be lifted and overwintered. Produces yellow-throated, tangerine-orange flowers atop grey-green foliage. Height: 90cm. Sun.

Elephant Ears 'Black Magic'
A great feature plant with rich burgundy, tropical-like foliage. Protect from hot sun and wind and bring indoors to overwinter. Height: 1–2m. Shade to A.M. sun.

PERENNIALS

Delphinium
Delphinium 'Blushing Bride'
A strong-stemmed variety with an upright habit. Spiked, pink flowers bloom in summer. More tolerant of heat and humidity than other varieties and retains flower colour. Divide every 3–4 years and cut back after flowering for new flush of growth. Prefers fertile, well-drained, moist soil. Height: 1–2m; width: 90cm. Sun to P.M. sun.

ROSES

'Quadra' Explorer *Hybrid Kordesii*
An impressive climbing rose producing double, deep red buds opening to rich red, 8–9cm flowers in late June through summer. Light, sweet fragrance. Height: 1.5–2m; spread: 1m. Sun.

Yew 'Hicks'

TREES & SHRUBS

Caragana 'Walker'
Caragana arborescens
Graceful weeping branches and fern-like foliage make an attractive feature plant usually sold grafted to a single stem. Left unpruned, it crawls along the ground or spills over rocks and walls. Height: graft dependent; width: 2–3m. Sun.

Yew 'Hicks'
Taxus x *media* 'Hicksii'
Narrow when young, Hicks' width increases with age. Its columnar growth habit makes it great as a feature or hedge. Slow growing. Requires moist soil. Height: 3m; width: 1.5m in 10–12 years. Sun or shade.

Rose 'Quadra'

Elephant Ears 'Black Magic'

Garages & Tool Sheds

'Turkestan' burning bush is ideal as a foundation plant for buildings in shady spots.

We have a tool shed attached to our house in a narrow and shady side yard. The space around it is not very attractive and we would like to spruce it up and still have the entrance to the shed accessible. What grows here?

As you'll need to be able to get in and out of the shed frequently, choose plants that are not thorny and won't get unruly. You could plant a bed of woodland perennials, shade-loving annuals and some shrubs along the edges of the area with a path leading through it to the shed door. This bed may even inspire you to fix up the shed itself and make it a featured destination in its own right.

Annuals

Begonia, Prelude Series

Outstanding, compact fibrous begonias for borders with masses of 2cm flowers all season long. Available in a mix, pink, scarlet and white. Performs well in shaded areas and will tolerate more sun if kept moist. Height: 15cm. Shade to A.M. sun.

Begonia 'Pin-Up Rose'

A tuberous begonia with stunning single, 9cm, picotee flowers in pure white or soft pink with bold rose margins and yellow centres. Height: 20–25cm. Shade to A.M. sun.

PERENNIALS

Astilbe
Astilbe x *rosea* 'Peach Blossom'
Great for a damp woodland or water-side garden, this heavy feeder produces fragrant, soft peach-pink plumes in summer. Clump-forming habit. Thrives in moist, fertile, organic, alkaline-free soil. Tolerates sun in a boggy site. Height: 45–60cm; width: 30–45cm. Shade to A.M. sun.

Hosta
Hosta 'Christmas Tree'
Produces a nice, medium-sized mound of wavy green foliage with creamy-white margins in a fairly short period of time. Thrives in moist, fertile, well-drained, organic, slightly acidic soil. Height: 60cm; width: 1.5m. Shade to A.M. sun.

Tibetan Primrose
Primula florindae
The largest primrose with fragrant, rosette-forming, sulphur-yellow flowers in summer. Requires moist, fertile, well-drained, organic soil. Height: 60–90cm; width: 30–45cm. Shade to A.M. sun.

TREES & SHRUBS

Burning Bush 'Turkestan'
Euonymus nanus var. *turkestanicus*
A versatile shrub. Bleeding heart-like, pink-and-orange blooms in summer with flaming red fall colour. Prefers moist, well-drained soil. Height: 1–1.5m; width: 1.5–2m. Sun or shade.

Hemlock 'Jeddeloh'
Tsuga canadensis
Bright green needles on a very nice nest-like, dwarf form. Requires moist, acidic soil. Height: 60–75cm; width: 90–100cm in 10–15 years. Shade to A.M. sun.

Begonia 'Pin-Up Rose'

Astilbe 'Peach Blossom'

Hosta 'Christmas Tree'

Tibetan Primrose

4

A Private
Paradise

…your own island of peace and serenity….

The one thing lacking in many of today's urban yards is privacy. The reality is that homes have been pushed closer together as lot sizes shrink, and the inevitable outcome has been a loss of personal space. While you can't change the size of your lot once it's been established, you can take steps to ensure the space you do have forms your own island of peace and serenity.

In my own yard, for example, I have a sheltered deck that is, for the most part, quite private. However, one spot offered a direct sightline into my neighbour's living room. I didn't want to infringe upon his privacy any more than he wanted to infringe on mine

I'm not averse to trying out-of-the-ordinary methods, and this problem called for a fairly innovative approach. I came up with a simple solution: I put two large containers on the deck and planted a six-foot Brandon cedar in each one, positioning them to screen the view. This is not a generally recommended solution for Zone 3 where I live—the fluctuating winter temperatures, combined with the limited insulating capacity of soil in a container, play havoc on a plant's roots. But I was prepared to take a chance and do the extra work of keeping the containers well watered to achieve my goal.

The cedars have not only taken care of the privacy issue; they look great on the deck, softening its hard, angular lines. What began as a problem turned out to be a perfect opportunity to add interest to the deck.

Of course, this solution is particularly tailored to my own gardening style—I don't mind spending a few dollars for the sake of expediency or trying something unconventional. Privacy is priceless. So go ahead, try something different and defend your turf—your way! ❧

Create and preserve privacy on your deck by mounting lattice panels for annual and perennial vines to climb.

I have a raised deck that is in full view of my neighbour's window. I would really like to give us both some privacy. What grows here?

I F YOU HAVE A FEW METRES of available space between your deck and the fence, there are narrow, tall trees that will provide you with the privacy you desire. Or you can attach lattice screening to the deck and plant annual or perennial climbers. If you only need screening when you are seated, consider building raised planters on the deck and filling them with taller annuals.

PERENNIALS

Big Petal Clematis
Clematis macropetala 'Jan Lindmark'
Produces a lush, pest-free screen; very hardy; attractive seedheads. Grow as a climber, groundcover or trailing over stone walls. Bell-shaped, mauve-purple flowers in spring. Fertile, well-drained soil. Height: 2–2.5m; width: 1–2m. Sun to P.M. sun.

Common Hops
Humulus lupulus
This vigorous climbing vine covers a large area and requires a strong support. Cone-like, green female flowers in summer. Cut back in fall. Prefers well-drained, organic, moderately fertile, moist soil. Height: 4–6m; width: 2–3+m. Sun to A.M. sun.

TREES & SHRUBS

Cedar 'Emerald Green'
Thuja occidentalis 'Smaragd'
Beautiful emerald-green foliage on
a very compact, pyramidal form that
fits well in tight spaces. Makes a striking feature tree. Height: 3–4m; width:
1–2m. A.M. sun.

Chokecherry
Prunus virginiana
A colourful tree that provides contrast
in small yards. This slow-growing,
dwarf form has pretty, clustered, white
blooms in spring, followed by edible,
blackish-blue fruit. Green leaves turn
a deep reddish-purple in early summer
and have a lovely purple fall colour.
Height: 4m; width: 4m. Sun.

Hawthorn 'Snowbird'
Crataegus x *mordenensis*
Great for small yards, screens or near
decks as it is fruitless and almost spine-
less. White, fragrant, double blooms
appear in spring. Height: 6m; width:
4–5m. Sun to P.M. sun.

Cedar 'Emerald Green'

Hawthorn 'Snowbird'

Chokecherry 'Bailey Select Schubert'

Common Hops

Lilac 'Dapple Dawn'

Syringa 'Aucubaefolia'

A very unique lilac with green-and-gold variegated foliage that is showy even when not in bloom. Large clusters of bluish-purple blooms in May on a spreading form. Height: 3m; width: 3m. Sun.

Mountain Ash 'Columnar European'

Sorbus aucuparia 'Fastigiata'

Also known as 'Pyramidal,' this is a great screening tree with an upright, columnar form. Slow growing with a dense growth habit. White blooms in spring are followed by big clusters of red berries. Requires well-drained soil. Height: 6–7m; width: 2–3m. Sun.

Ornamental Crabapple 'Thunderchild Columnar'

Malus x *pumila*

This unique columnar form has many uses in the landscape: plant a few in a

Mountain Ash 'Columnar European'

Poplar 'Tower'

row for a narrow screen or use to high-light entrances, driveways and sunny side yards. Displays deep burgundy-purple foliage and abundant pink blooms in spring. Height: 3m in 5–6 years; width: 30–60cm. Sun.

Pine 'Columnar Scotch'

Pinus sylvestris 'Fastigiata'

Very dense foliage with a rich, steely-blue colour on a very narrow form. Hardy and drought tolerant. Height: 7–9m; width: 45–60cm. Sun.

Poplar 'Tower'

Populus x *canescens*

Stately screen or tall, semi-formal hedge, this tree is perfect for small yards and does not sucker. Fast growing with an extremely upright growth habit. Height: 20m; width: 2–3m. Sun.

Pine 'Columnar Scotch'

Ornamental Crabapple 'Thunderchild Columnar'

Dense plants like 'Woodwardii' cedar can help filter the sounds of traffic at street level.

The front yard of our bungalow faces a noisy, busy street and we would like to use plants to filter out the sound. What grows here?

AN ATTRACTIVE, DEEP BORDER of plants will do quite a bit to filter the noise at ground level and slightly above. Use plants that are dense and, if blocking noise is not just a seasonal concern, be sure to mix in some evergreens. Remember that these plants may be exposed to street pollution, salt and heavy snow load, so choose accordingly. Elevating the bed will help to block the noise further while lifting the shorter plants out of harms way.

ANNUALS

Petunia, Tidal Wave Series

This series is colourful and versatile—it can be grown as a spreading ground-cover or tall hedge, depending on how closely you space the plants. Spacing 30cm apart results in plants growing up to 90cm tall. Spacing 60–75cm apart results in plants spreading to 90cm. Flowers are large and bright. Sun to P.M. sun.

PERENNIALS

Culver's Root
Veronicastrum virginicum

Adds height to a mixed border and interesting texture with its whorls of leaves. Clump-forming and upright in habit. Spiked, white to pink or bluish-purple flowers in summer. Tolerates some dryness, but prefers moist, fertile, organic soil. Height: 60–180cm; width: 45cm. Sun to P.M. sun.

TREES & SHRUBS

Barberry 'Ruby Carousel'
Berberis thunbergii var. *atropurpurea* 'Bailone'

Dense and very thorny in habit—great as a living barrier in a formal or informal hedge. Bright yellow blooms in May–June followed by bright red berries. Beautiful reddish-purple foliage with a uniform growth habit. Height: 90–100cm; width: 100cm. Sun.

Cedar 'Woodwardii'
Thuja occidentalis

This hardy, globe-shaped cedar holds its dense, deep green foliage to the ground and looks great in large beds and rock gardens. Best shaped annually. Height: 2m; width: 2–3m. Sun to P.M. sun.

Currant 'Alpine'
Ribes alpinum

Lustrous, bright green foliage on a fast-growing shrub; popular for hedging. Prune regularly to maintain a dense form. Height: 1.5m; width: 1.5m. Sun.

Wayfaring Tree 'Emerald Triumph'
Viburnum lantana

This versatile shrub makes a superb screen, mixing well in shrub borders. Pretty white blooms appear in spring, followed by pink fruit that matures to purple-black. Leathery leaves turn rich red in fall. Height: 1.5m; width: 1.5m. Sun to P.M. sun.

Currant 'Alpine'

Barberry 'Ruby Carousel'

Petunias (L–R) 'Tidal Wave Cherry, Silver & Purple'

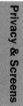

A densely planted mixed bed will discourage trespassers and can add beauty to the landscape all year long.

We have a sunny corner lot and the neighbourhood children are always cutting across the lawn. I would like to replace the trampled section of lawn with a bed that discourages trespassing. What grows here?

A CAREFULLY POSITIONED garden bed will not only block access, but will act as an attractive feature to frame and highlight your lot. Plant densely, with a mix of deciduous and evergreen plants to deter trespassers in all seasons. Consider this bed from all angles, remembering that you will see it as you approach the house and quite likely from any front windows within your home.

ANNUALS

Four O'clocks

Also known as Marvel of Peru. Ideal in backgrounds or as an annual hedge. Fragrant flowers open in the afternoon. Unique, 5cm, trumpet-shaped flowers available in red, white, yellow, pink and violet. Very heat tolerant. Height: up to 60cm; spacing: 30–40cm. Sun.

PERENNIALS

Checker Mallow
Sidalcea candida

A clump-forming perennial with an upright habit. Produces spikes of white flowers in summer. Prefers moist, well-drained, fertile, deep soil—avoid winter wet. Protect with snow in winter. Height: 60–90cm; width: 45–60cm. Sun to P.M. sun.

Mugwort
Artemisia vulgaris
'Oriental Limelight'

A tough, upright accent plant for difficult spots—extremely tolerant of hot and dry sites. Prune hard in spring. Dense, variegated, cream-and-green foliage. Prefers well-drained, alkaline, poor, dry soil. Height: 60–170cm; width: 30–100cm. Sun to P.M. sun.

Checker Mallow

Mugwort 'Oriental Limelight'

Four O'clocks

ROSES

'Dart's Dash'
Hybrid Rugosa

A dense shrub rose that puts on a great display of red hips in the fall. Hardy to Zone 2. Semi-double, purple-crimson, 8–10cm flowers bloom all summer with a strong, sweet fragrance. Height: 1m; spread: 1m. Sun.

'George Vancouver' Explorer
Shrub

Clustered blooms are followed by hundreds of red rosehips in fall. Good resistance to mildew and blackspot and hardy to Zone 3. Semi-double, medium red, 6cm flowers bloom June through summer with a light fragrance. Height: 60–75cm; spread: 60–75cm. Sun.

TREES & SHRUBS

Barberry 'Sunsation'
Berberis thunbergii 'Monry'

Striking planted en masse or used as a contrast or hedging shrub. Golden, glowing foliage matures to an orange cast on this compact, upright and vase-shaped plant. Produces greenish-yellow berries. Height: 90–100cm; width: 100cm. Sun.

Rose 'George Vancouver'

Barberry 'Sunsation'

Rose 'Dart's Dash'

Caragana 'Pygmy'

Spiraea 'Dart's Red'

Caragana 'Pygmy'

Caragana pygmaea

Makes a great small and formal hedge. Good for hot, dry locations. 'Pygmy' has a naturally vase-shaped form. Height: 1m; width: 1m. Sun to P.M. sun.

Juniper 'Blue Carpet'

Juniperus squamata

This juniper's intense blue foliage makes it an excellent feature or contrast plant. Lovely draping over rocks and walls, as well as bordering shrub beds. Very attractive groundcover. Height: 15cm; width: 2m. Sun.

Sea Buckthorn

Hippophae rhamnoides

The female plant has masses of bright orange berries in fall, lasting all winter. Can be a grown as a small tree or shrub. Displays dense, willow-like, silvery-grey foliage. Height: 3–6m; width: 3–6m. Sun.

Spiraea 'Dart's Red'

Spiraea japonica

A pretty spiraea, with dense, rich bluish-green foliage that turns a lovely reddish-purple colour in fall. Deep purple-pink blooms appear in June and July. Height: 90–100cm; width: 90–100cm. Sun to P.M. sun.

Sea Buckthorn

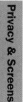

'Donald Wyman' lilac is a great screening plant with lovely spring blooms as a bonus.

The side of my yard faces a busy pedestrian walkway. I do have a fence, but would like to make this area more private and less visible to passers-by. What grows here?

IF SPACE ALLOWS, consider planting columnar or smaller, canopied trees to increase your privacy. Extend the height of your fence by attaching lattice panels or, as one of our intrepid staff did, attaching a series of arches from post to post and growing vines up the fence and arch. You can also mount window boxes near the top of the fence and fill them with taller annuals.

ANNUALS

Petunia, Double Wave Series
Lovely 5–8cm double flowers in wonderful colour shades on plants that easily fill hanging baskets and containers. Spreads 60–90cm. Sun.

PERENNIALS

Clematis
Clematis macropetala
'Markham's Pink'
Produces a lush, pest-free and very hardy screen that requires support. Grow as a climber, groundcover or trail over stone walls. Do not cut back. Pink-mauve flowers in spring are followed by attractive seed heads. Prefers fertile, well-drained soil and cool roots. Height: 3–5m; width: 75–90cm. Sun to P.M. sun.

Honeysuckle 'Belgica Select'

Lonicera perclymenum

This twining vine displays lovely, scented, pink, yellow and red blooms June through summer; requires support. Flowers attract hummingbirds. Can be grown as a groundcover. Height: 5–6m; width: 1m. Sun to P.M. sun.

ROSES

'Martin Frobisher' Explorer

Hybrid Rugosa

A pillar-shaped shrub with erect canes covered in reddish bark. Hardy to Zone 2. Blooms profusely all summer with double, soft pink, 5–6cm flowers that have a light fragrance. Height: 2m; spread: 2m. Sun.

Nannyberry

Cedar 'Techny'

TREES & SHRUBS

Lilac 'Donald Wyman'

Syringa x *prestoniae*

A non-suckering variety that can be trained to tree form. Single, lightly scented, dark purple blooms in long clusters present late in the season. Height: 3–4m; width: 3–4m. Sun to P.M. sun.

Cedar 'Techny'

Thuja occidentalis 'Mission'

This hardy cedar is excellent as a hedge or feature tree and is very tolerant of shearing and shaping. Dark green foliage looks coarse when young. Slow-growing. Height: 3–5m; width: 2m. Sun to P.M. sun.

Nannyberry

Viburnum lentago

Lustrous, compact, dark green foliage highlights creamy-white blooms in June. Edible, blue-black fruits are excellent for jams and jellies. Height: 4–5m; width: 2–3m. Sun or shade.

Petunia 'Double Wave Pink'

Rose 'Martin Frobisher'

A few well-placed trees like 'Paper' birch can both create privacy and add to the view.

Our house backs out onto a breezy, man-made lake around which there is a public footpath. We need some privacy but don't want to obscure the great view. What grows here?

YOU NEED TO ASK yourself where you need the most privacy and which views of the lake you are not willing to sacrifice. If there is a conflict, you have some tough decisions to make. Compromise and plant very open-headed trees that afford for both screening and a view, and underplant with a variety of other plants. If your lot slopes down to the water, you may be able to create a privacy screen of dense hedging at the bottom end of the yard.

TREES & SHRUBS

Birch 'Paper'
Betula papyrifera
Beautiful feature tree for large yards and parks. Spectacular in winter with hoar frost on thousands of small branches. A large, oval-headed tree with attractive bright white bark that often peels. Produces catkins in spring. Height: 15–20m; width: 10–15m. Sun.

Juniper 'Moonglow'
Juniperus scopulorum

Makes a great feature plant or screen that requires no shearing or pruning. A dense, pyramidal form with intense bluish-grey foliage. Height: 6m; width: 1.5m. Sun.

Lilac 'James MacFarlane'
Syringa x *prestoniae*

Dark green foliage highlights masses of rich pink, single blooms in spring. A non-suckering variety that can be pruned to an open form. Height: 3–4m; width: 3–4m. Sun to P.M. sun.

Mountain Ash 'Showy'
Sorbus decora

Sometimes sold as 'Grootendorst,' this dense, round-headed tree has foliage that contrasts well with clustered, white spring blooms and red fruit. Great for small yards. A very hardy and fireblight resistant variety. Requires well-drained soil. Height: 6–7m; width: 4–5m. Sun.

Ornamental Crabapple 'Makamik'
Malus

This open-headed tree is spectacular in bloom. Bronze leaves set off dark red flower buds that open to purple-red blooms, followed by 1–2cm, purple-red fruit. Blooms in May or early June. Height: 10m; width: 10m. Sun.

Wayfaring Tree 'Mohican'
Viburnum lantana

A compact form that is great for screening. Creamy-white blooms appear in May and green foliage turns purple-red in fall. Height: 2–3m; width: 2–3m. Sun.

Juniper 'Moonglow'

Lilac 'James MacFarlane'

Ornamental Crabapple 'Makamik'

Fast-growing trees like 'Lodgepole' pine can both provide privacy year round and are attractive additions to any large yard.

Our acreage is not in a sub-division and, although our nearest neighbour is some distance away, we would like fast-growing plants to provide more privacy. Space is not an issue. What grows here?

Trees that grow quickly often have a short lifespan. Use these trees to achieve quick results, but work some slower-growing species into your landscaping plan that, in time, will add to the beauty and privacy of your property. There is nothing wrong with planting a traditional windbreak, but using a combination of trees will help to protect against losing the whole tree line to a potential insect, disease or drought problem.

Trees & Shrubs

Maple 'Sensation'
Acer negundo
An extremely hardy tree with bright green foliage touched with a powdery-blue coating on the stems and buds. Beautiful, brilliant red colour in fall. 'Sensation' has a slow but uniform growth habit. Height: 7–10m; width: 6–7m. Sun.

Oak 'Burr'

Quercus macrocarpa

A wide, pyramid-shaped, hardy, slow-growing oak—well suited to large yards. Should be thought of as a heritage tree and planted where it can be enjoyed for generations. Adaptable to wet or dry sites. Prefers acidic soil. Height: 20–25m; width: 9–10m. Sun.

Pine 'Lodgepole'

Pinus contorta var. *latifolia*

A tidy tree that doesn't drop cones and is very attractive planted in groups. A narrow form with a beautiful straight trunk. Height: 20m; width: 4–6m. Sun.

Poplar 'Brooks #6'

Populus

Ideal for large spaces or shelterbelts. This seedless variety has dark green, leathery foliage. Very vigorous and fast growing. Height: 15–20m; width: 15–20m. Sun.

Spruce 'Fat Albert'

Picea pungens

Very dense, bright blue foliage on a broad pyramidal form—a perfect feature tree for large yards. Height: 15–20m; width: 6–9m. Sun to P.M. sun.

Spruce 'Rubra Spicata'

Picea abies

Great for large spaces—a unique, fast-growing feature or showy background tree. Spectacular when bright red new growth is opening up. Height: 4m; width: 2m in 15 years. Sun.

Spruce 'Rubra Spicata'

Oak 'Burr'

Spruce 'Fat Albert'

5
Marking Your Territory

…more psychological than practical…

Sometimes I wonder what the urban landscape would look like if we lived in a world without fences. Lawns would run in great swaths, trees would grow together to form lush canopies and waves of tulips and narcissus would flow beyond the confines of their beds and across property lines.

And then the cold reality sets in. Most people see to prefer to live in a world sharply delineated by border after border, fence after fence. Well, if I have to mark my territory, then I'm at least going to create a border I can live with.

I'm not a big fan of conventional fences, so when one of the fences bordering a neighbour's yard started to deteriorate, I used the opportunity to plant a living fence of Techny cedars. The cedars create a lush boundary that provides virtually all the benefits of a standard fence without the cold feeling of traditional "dead" fences.

Proponents of the conventional approach might scoff at this idea. After all, fences are meant to give the homeowner privacy, and to keep his pets and small children in the yard while keeping outsiders (whether human or animal) out. But in reality, fences have a mixed record at meeting these goals. Cats still climb fences, dogs dig underneath them and most able-bodied people have no problem hopping a fence, either to invade your privacy or to escape a boring dinner party. As far as I'm concerned, the exclusionary nature of fences is more psychological than practical, and they do little to foster a sense of community. In fact, on one side of my house I don't have a fence at all. My neighbour and I share a stand of trees, a mini-forest that hides the property line somewhere within its depths, and it serves its purpose just fine.

Plants can provide privacy while at the same time giving the neighbours something to appreciate. My Techny cedars can be admired from both sides of the fence. And for those times where I don't feel like being neighbourly, they do provide some separation and privacy screening. I chose the Technys because they're dense enough to prevent errant soccer balls and stray dogs from intruding, but don't slam the door on my neighbour.

And there are other advantages. First of all, the cedars look far better than any conventional fence, and once well established they need next to no pruning, fertilizer or water. I'll never need to buy paint, nails or two-by-fours to keep my cedar fence healthy. In the long run, I'll have something not only more beautiful, but considerably more valuable than a cold barrier of stone, metal or wood.

They say that good fences make good neighbours, and perhaps they do—if you mark your territory in a way that not only meets your needs and those of the people around you, but also enhances the landscape. ✂

When considering planting a living fence, don't overlook annuals like 'Silver Cup' lavatera.

We have a sunny front yard and want to mark the property line with plants. What grows here?

A LIVING FENCE is a planting that runs in a narrow strip defining a boundary. It can consist of traditional hedging material pruned to a formal shape, or less conventionally used plants spaced closely in a single row. Seasonal living fences are comprised of thick plantings of annuals or perennials that are only visible during spring and summer and offer no winter presence. Each of these interpretations requires different amounts of maintenance.

ANNUALS

Lavatera 'Silver Cup'

Grow in a row to create a low, compact hedge. These bushy plants produce satiny, rose, cup-shaped flowers—very impressive in the garden. Great in mass displays. Height: 60–90cm. Sun.

PERENNIALS

Peony

Paeonia officinalis
'Anemoniflora Rosea'

This variety is generally more compact, blooms earlier and has thicker stems which hold up better to adverse weather conditions. Single, pinkish-red flowers with yellow stamens bloom in spring. Clump-forming habit. Moist, fertile, well-drained soil. Plant eyes 5cm deep or less. Height: 60–70cm; width: 60–90cm. Sun to P.M. sun.

ROSES

'Adelaide Hoodless' Parkland
Hardy Shrub

Another Canadian rose introduction that is hardy to Zone 2 with snow cover. Double, red, 7cm flowers from June to frost in clusters of up to 25. Light fragrance. Height: 1.5–2m; spread: 1.5–2m. Sun.

'Morden Blush' Parkland
Hardy Shrub

Blooms profusely from June to frost in clusters of up to five. Double, ivory with blush-pink centres, 7–8cm flowers. Softly fragrant. Hardy to Zone 2. Height: 60–90cm; spread: 60–90cm. Sun.

Rose 'Morden Blush'

Rose 'Adelaide Hoodless'

Peony 'Anemoniflora Rosea'

'Morden Centennial' Parkland
Hardy Shrub

A very showy rose. Lightly fragrant, double, bright pink, 7–8cm flowers bloom repeatedly through summer. Hardy to Zone 2. Height: 1–1.5m; spread: 1–1.5m. Sun.

TREES & SHRUBS

Cedar 'Danica'
Thuja occidentalis

Bright green foliage, tinged blue in winter, on a round, compact form that makes a lovely, slow-growing informal hedge. Great in rock gardens. Height: 45cm; width: 45–60cm in 20 years. Sun to P.M. sun.

Cotoneaster 'Hedge'
Cotoneaster acutifolius

Also known as 'Peking,' this very hardy and useful shrub is traditionally sheared and shaped for formal hedging, but is equally attractive left to arch in its natural form. Plant 30–45cm apart for hedges. Dark green, dense foliage turns a lovely orange-red colour in fall. Height: 2–3m; width: 2–3m. Sun to P.M. sun.

Rose 'Morden Centennial'

Mockorange 'Miniature Snowflake'

Currant 'Alpine'

Currant 'Alpine'
Ribes alpinum

Lustrous, bright green foliage on a fast-growing shrub, popular for hedging. Prune regularly to maintain a dense form. Height: 1.5m; width: 1.5m. Sun.

Mockorange 'Miniature Snowflake'
Philadelphus

Great as an informal hedge or feature shrub. Prolific, double, white, fragrant blooms appear in June. Height: 60–90cm; width: 30–60cm. Sun to P.M. sun.

Spiraea 'Tor'
Spiraea betulifolia

This shrub may not look like much at the nursery, but it makes a lovely informal hedge with clustered, creamy-white blooms in June and striking fall colours of gold, orange and bronze. Great in borders. Height: 60–75cm; width: 60–75cm. Sun to P.M. sun.

Cedar 'Danica'

Cotoneaster 'Hedge'

Oriental poppy is an old-fashioned favourite that is a perfect complement to the traditional picket fence.

We have a traditional, low, white picket fence around our sunny front yard. It is set back about 60cm from the lot line on all sides. We'd like to grow plants on both sides of it. What grows here?

CONSIDER A COTTAGE garden look—not only can you grow plants on either side of the fence, but you can also train the plants to grow on the fence itself, adding to the charm of your yard. Choose plants with vividly coloured blooms that will stand out against the white pickets.

ANNUALS

Snapdragon, Rocket Series

Snapdragons are an old-fashioned favourite available in a wide range of colours. The Rocket series features extra-long flower spikes that make excellent cutflowers. Frost tolerant. Height: 90cm. Sun.

Trachelium 'Devotion Blue'

Excellent in containers and flowerbeds, as well as a superb cutflower. Masses of small, delicate, clustered flowers bloom in shades of lavender-blue. Height: 30–40cm; spacing: 20–25cm. Sun to P.M. sun.

PERENNIALS

Oriental Poppy
Papaver orientale

Huge, papery poppies with black stamens in a wide colour range bloom in late spring to early summer. This clump-forming plant is summer dormant, so pair with baby's breath or any other late-blooming perennial to fill in gaps. Dislikes being moved. Best in a sunny, dry location and fertile, well-drained soil. Height: 50–60cm; width: 45–60cm. Sun to P.M. sun.

Painted Daisy
Tanacetum coccineum

Pretty, single, daisy-like, pink flowers with yellow centres bloom on this upright perennial in early summer. Prefers well-drained soil. Height: 45–75cm; width: 30–45cm. Sun to P.M. sun.

Painted Daisy

Trachelium 'Devotion Blue'

ROSES

'Morden Fireglow' Parkland
Hardy Shrub

A rare shade in hardy shrub roses. Double, scarlet-orange, 6–8cm flowers bloom in June, repeating in summer. Lightly fragrant. Hardy to Zone 2. Height: 60–90cm; spread: 60–90cm. Sun.

TREES & SHRUBS

Spiraea 'Little Princess'
Spiraea japonica

A small, rounded and compact form of spiraea that is attractive near the front to middle of borders. Fast growing with good red fall colour. Pretty, bright pink blooms in summer. Height: 60–75cm; width: 90–100cm. Sun to P.M. sun.

Weigela 'Minuet'
Weigela florida

Striking ruby-red to pink, yellow-throated, lightly scented blooms in early summer. Provides great contrast. Dark green, purple-tinted leaves. Plant where snow collects. Height: 60–90cm; width: 90cm. Sun.

Weigela 'Minuet'

Spiraea 'Little Princess'

Hedges & Fences

'Cuthbertson Floribunda Mix' sweet peas effectively provide both privacy and fragrant coverage on a chain-link fence.

I have a chain-link fence separating my yard from my neighbours' on both sides. I would like to grow plants that will create a privacy screen in specific areas of my garden. Because of space limitations, the plants must be compact and able to grow close to the fence or on it. What grows here?

ETERMINE WHERE PRIVACY is required most. Do you want to screen your patio or perhaps block the view of your neighbour's parking pad? Place the tallest plants in front of those areas. Alternatively, use an assortment of climbing plants on the fence and place dense plants in front of it.

ANNUALS

Cup and Saucer Vine 'Purple'
Cobaea scandens
A fast-growing annual vine that is wind tolerant. Large flowers open light green maturing to purple and are cup shaped. Height: up to 3m; spacing: 25–30cm. Sun.

Sweet Pea, Cuthbertson Floribunda Series
This series blooms prolifically with sweetly-scented flowers borne on long stems making excellent cutflowers. Available in maroon, rose-pink, scarlet, white and mix. Requires support. Height: 2m. Sun.

PERENNIALS

Delphinium, Clansman Series
Delphinium
This heavy feeder has an upright habit and may require staking. Plant in a wind-sheltered location. Produces spiked flowers in a variety of colours in summer. Divide every 3–4 years. Prefers moist, fertile, well-drained soil. Height: 1–1.5m; width: 75–90cm. Sun to A.M. sun.

Vine Bower
Clematis viticella 'Polish Spirit'
Makes a hardy, lush, pest-free and easy-to-grow screen. It needs a support and cool roots. Purple-blue flowers in summer are followed by very attractive seed heads. Cut back in late fall. Thrives in fertile, well-drained soil. Height: 2.5–3m; width: 1–2m. Sun to P.M. sun.

TREES & SHRUBS

Cedar 'Rushmore'
Thuja occidentalis 'Rushmore'
Excellent for framing a site or for use as a screen in a space-restricted area. Soft green, windburn-resistant foliage covers a narrow, upright form. Height: 4m; width: 1m in 10–12 years. Sun to P.M. sun.

VEGETABLES

Jerusalem Artichoke
Very easy to grow and extremely hardy. Produces chocolate-scented, ornamental, yellow blooms and delicious, small, potato-like tubers with a crisp, nutty flavour. Harvest like potatoes, but in both early spring and late in summer. Height: 1.5+m. Sun.

Cup and Saucer Vine 'Purple'

Jerusalem Artichoke

Vine Bower 'Polish Spirit'

6
On the Small &
Narrow

…come to terms with reality…

In my modern urban yard, it would be difficult to enjoy the massive maples of my childhood farm. The huge, overgrown canopy would reduce my limited space to a dark, shadowy cavern. I sometimes regret their absence, but I've had to come to terms with reality. Unfortunately, many homeowners haven't.

As Bob Dylan trenchantly observed, the times are a-changing. Rapid urbanization in North America has led to big homes being built on standard lots. Plants that suited the large lots of yesteryear are simply not sensible choices for today's postage-stamp yards. Even if you are lucky enough to own a spacious yard, most landscapes have at least one tight or narrow spot that must be dealt with. I, like many other gardeners, literally cringe when I see magnificent trees, lovingly tended for years, chopped down or topped to tortured forms because the person who planted them didn't consider their final size.

Like it or not, most of today's homeowners must choose from a different list of plants, plants that will fit comfortably within the confines of the yard when they reach their maximum size. Fortunately, that list boasts many terrific choices. With a little imagination and the right plants, you can create a tiny masterpiece.

Plant breeders have put a lot of energy into developing specialty forms of many of the old favourites. There are dwarf apple trees, cedars, yews and pines. Columnar varieties are available in many species, from poplars to spruces, and miniature roses, rhododendrons and petunias are now appearing. These plants are just as beautiful and functional as the full-sized favourites, producing gorgeous blooms and delicious fruit, but they're also practical for the modern yard, growing at a rate that allows for moderate pruning and maintenance. The lazy gardener in me is thrilled at the prospect of not having to spend my time hacking back shrubs to keep them in check and growing to their full potential.

But I still miss those maples. ⚘

Japanese tree lilac is an attractive choice for smaller yards and blooms at a time of year when most trees have already finished.

I have a two-storey condominium and would like to landscape the small backyard with plants that are in proportion to the building, but that won't outgrow the space. What grows here?

SOME CONDOMINIUM associations have strict planting regulations, so be sure to first check on size and planting restrictions. Following that, choose from the numerous small and narrow trees, as well as large perennials that are available. These should relate well to the building's size and still leave you with space to add smaller plants and address additional considerations, such as a patio, walkway or play area.

PERENNIALS

Tawny Foxtail Lily
Eremurus stenophyllus

This upright plant has interesting and unusual flower spikes that bloom in shades of yellow to orange in early summer. As the plant goes dormant in mid summer, fill in the gaps with late-blooming perennials. Resents being moved. Prefers a sheltered location with fertile, well-drained, moist soil a little on the sandy side—avoid wet sites. Height: 90–100cm; width: 30–45cm. Sun.

Tawny Foxtail Lily

Martagon Lily
Lilium martagon 'Claude Shride'

Martagon lilies are tall, elegant plants with masses of tiny blooms. This variety has recurved, grey-purple flowers with yellow spots in late spring—lovely in bouquets. They prefer a partially shaded, moist location in cool, well-drained, organic soil. Height: 90–100cm; width: 30–45cm. Filtered P.M. sun.

TREES & SHRUBS

Birch 'Young's Weeping'
Betula pendula 'Youngii'

A strongly weeping tree that needs training to achieve a specific height, at which point it will weep down and may even cover the ground. This species is often grafted on a 1.5–2.5m single stem. Makes a beautiful feature in small yards; has bright white bark and produces soft catkins in spring. Height: training dependent; spread: 3m. Sun.

Martagon Lily 'Claude Shride'

Birch 'Young's Weeping'

Caragana 'Sutherland'
Caragana arborescens

Great for dry sites, this very narrow, up-right caragana is also a good feature tree for small yards. Produces yellow blooms in May. Height: 4–5m; width: 1m. Sun.

Japanese Tree Lilac
Syringa reticulata

A lovely tree for small yards; blooms when most trees have finished. Produces creamy-white to yellow flowers in summer. Very slow-growing, maintaining an oval shape for many years before widening. Easily pruned and shaped. Usually sold in a multi-stemmed form. Height: 10m; width: 10m. Sun.

Juniper 'Mountbatten'
Juniperus chinensis

A fast-growing juniper that requires little shearing or pruning to maintain a compact pyramidal form. Rich blu-ish-green foliage highlights abundant berries. Height: 3–4m; width: 2m. Sun to P.M. sun.

Ornamental Crabapple 'Rosthern Columnar'
Malus baccata 'Columnaris'

One of the most columnar flowering crabapples available (also known as 'Siberian'). In May, it is covered in masses of white blooms followed by yellow-checkered, red fruit. Great feature tree for small yards. Height: 6m; width: 1.5–2m. Sun.

Pine 'Columnar Scotch'
Pinus sylvestris 'Fastigiata'

Very dense foliage with a rich, steely-blue colour on a very narrow form. Hardy and drought tolerant. Height: 7–9m; width: 45–60cm. Sun.

Caragana 'Sutherland'

Ornamental Crabapple 'Rosthern Columnar'

Pine 'Columnar White'
Pinus strobus 'Fastigiata'
An upright, narrow form that is
very useful for small yards. Beautiful
silver-blue foliage contrasts nicely with
darker evergreens. Height: 10m; width:
2–3m. Sun.

Pine 'Silver Whispers'
Pinus cembra 'Klein'
A perfectly-shaped, dwarf pyramidal
pine that is superb in shrub beds. Dark
green, silver-striped needles and purple
cones. Height: 4m; width: 2m in 15–20
years. Sun.

Spiraea 'Froebel'
Spiraea japonica 'Froebelii'
Use along walkways, driveways or in
shrub beds. Very showy, bright pink
flowers bloom in summer. Shear after
flowering to promote rebloom. New
growth is russet-red turning dark
green on this fast-growing, drought-
tolerant plant. Height: 90–100cm;
width: 90–100cm. Sun to P.M. sun.

Spiraea 'Froebel'

Pine 'Columnar Scotch'

Juniper 'Mountbatten'

'Tardiva' hydrangea is one of those versatile plants that adapts well to variations in sunlight.

The front yard of my townhouse is small, shady and bordered by a 2m high fence. I would like to make this space more attractive and welcoming as it serves as the main entrance to my home. What grows here?

YOU CAN MAKE A striking impression on visitors with the introduction of unique plants, a clearly-defined path and perhaps statuary. Plant large shrubs that can be trained to a small tree form and strategically place containers as needed until eye-catching perennials and shrubs reach a significant size. Use the fence as part of the landscape and grow plants up it or mount planters onto it. Consider taking a very simplified approach and use only one or two types of plants in several small groupings; the repeating design will be particularly effective in small, enclosed spaces.

ANNUALS

Begonia, Non-Stop Series

Bright, clear colours and stunning, large, double flowers make this series a winner. 'Appleblossom' has large, white and soft-pink bicolour, double flowers. Height: 20–25cm; spacing: 15–25cm. Shade to a.m. sun.

PERENNIALS

Hosta

Hosta 'Emerald Tiara'

Eye-catching gold-centred foliage with green edges on a hosta that requires 1–2 hours of direct sunlight per day to maintain its colour. Forms a dense mound. Requires moist, fertile, well-drained, slightly acidic soil. Height: 45cm; width: 90cm. Shade to A.M. sun.

Rayflower
Ligularia japonica

Deeply cut, large leaves on a clump-forming, upright plant. Clustered, daisy-like, yellow-orange flowers bloom in early summer. Avoid bright, windy sites. Prefers very moist, deep, moderately fertile soil. Height: 1–1.5m; width: 75–100cm. Shade to A.M. sun.

TREES & SHRUBS

Snowberry 'Marleen'
Symphoricarpos x doorenbosii

A very hardy shrub with a pendulous branching habit. Displays bluish leaves with pale pink blooms from June to September. Purplish fruits persist until November and can be used in arrangements. Height: 1m; width: 1m. Sun or shade.

Hydrangea 'Tardiva'
Hydrangea paniculata

A lovely accent shrub that does bloom in shade, but reaches its full potential with some direct sunlight. Beautiful clusters of white flowers bloom in August and mature to shades of pink. Requires moist soil. Height: 2–3m; width: 2–3m. Sun to P.M. sun.

Ninebark 'Tilden Parks'
Physocarpus opulifolius

A versatile plant that makes a dense, fast-growing groundcover. Great for erosion control on slopes. Height: 40–50cm; width: 60–100cm. Sun or shade.

Yew 'Taunton's Spreading'
Taxus x media 'Tauntonii'

This evergreen is globe shaped with a flat top. It spreads with age to form a lovely, windburn-resistant groundcover. Slow growing—requires little pruning. Height: 90–150cm; width: 1.5–2m. Shade to A.M. sun.

Rayflower

Hosta 'Emerald Tiara'

Yew 'Taunton's Spreading'

Begonia 'Non-Stop Appleblossom'

'Blue Bells' browallia's rounded form is particularly attractive in hanging baskets and containers, making it an excellent choice for decks and balconies.

We recently sold our home and moved to a second-floor apartment with a small, sheltered balcony. It is quite shady, only receiving light directly in the mornings. I miss growing plants in my old garden and would like to try some containers. What grows here?

THERE ARE NUMEROUS attractive styles and sizes of containers available that will allow you to still enjoy gardening on a smaller, more manageable scale. Choose larger containers to minimize drying out and always use good-quality potting soil. In cooler zones, annuals will be your only choice as perennials and shrubs will not overwinter reliably in containers. If your heart is set on trying these plants, give them away in the fall to a gardener who will appreciate them, to an organization such as Habitat for Humanity or to a school, community garden or church.

ANNUALS

Begonia 'Harmony Mix'
Outstanding compact fibrous begonia with masses of small flowers in a mix of pink, scarlet and white. Very uniform, free flowering and tolerant of rain and heat. Performs well in full shade, yet will tolerate more sun if kept moist. Height: 15cm. Shade to A.M. sun.

Browallia 'Blue Bells'

Excellent in hanging baskets and containers. Deep violet-purple, 3cm, bluebell-like flowers. Striking rounded bush habit. Height: 25–30cm; spacing: 15–20cm. Shade to A.M. sun.

English Ivy
Hedera helix

Adds great texture to mixed containers. Excellent in hanging baskets and planters. A wide range of types available with foliage differing in size, shape and colour. Trails to 60–90cm. Sun to A.M. sun.

Fuchsia 'Dark Eyes'

Excellent in hanging baskets and containers. These trailing plants produce colourful, exotic flowers. Best grown in sheltered locations. Height: varies; trails to 30–60cm. Shade to A.M. sun.

Lobelia, Regatta Series

Masses of tiny flowers make trailing lobelia a traditional favourite for hanging baskets and containers. Height: 7–10cm; trails to 30cm. A.M. or P.M. sun.

English Ivy

Fuchsia 'Dark Eyes'

Lobelia 'Regatta Sky-blue'

Begonia 'Harmony Mix'

Mass plantings are a very effective method of drawing the eye, even when composed entirely of common plants like Shasta Daisies.

I have a narrow side yard leading to my home's entrance that I want to make more welcoming. There is a sunny bed between the house and sidewalk that is 60cm wide by 6m long. I can't spend a lot on plants, but I really want impact. What grows here?

A MASS PLANTING of one type of plant will give you tremendous impact and, depending on the plant you choose, blooms and colour all season. If your budget is really restricted and you have the time and inclination, try growing annuals, perennials and even shrubs from seeds or cuttings. Or, if you can afford to buy plants, choose those that spread and fill in quickly or reseed themselves reliably. This location, because it is so well contained by the house and sidewalk, is a perfect spot for plants considered invasive or aggressive.

ANNUALS

African Daisy, Spring Flash Series
A very colourful addition to beds and borders, available in vibrant orange and yellow shades. Daisy-like, 8cm blooms cover these heat-tolerant plants. Height: 25–30cm. Sun.

PERENNIALS

Daylily
Hemerocallis 'Raspberry Pixie'
Fragrant, raspberry-red flowers bloom in July atop grass-like, mounding foliage. Considered an extended bloomer—flowers last longer than a single day. Prefers moist, fertile, well-drained soil. Height: 30cm; width: 30–60cm. Sun to P.M. sun.

Iceland Poppy
Papaver nudicaule

Poppies are versatile plants that are good for naturalizing woodland or sunny areas. They self-sow freely. Deadhead to prolong blooming. Various colours are available. Papery-thin flowers bloom from spring to fall. Height: 30–45cm; width: 15–30cm. Sun to P.M. sun.

Perennial Blue Flax
Linum perenne

A clump-forming plant covered in striking but dainty, sky-blue flowers that last one day each, produced over a long period in summer. Allow to self-seed. Prefers moist, well-drained soil. Height: 40–60cm; width: 30–45cm. Sun to P.M. sun.

Shasta Daisy
Leucanthemum x *superbum* 'Alaska'

A traditional shasta prized for its single, white flowers with yellow centres that bloom late spring to fall. Benefits from deadheading and its blooms make good cutflowers. Best divided every 2–3 years. Prefers moist, well-drained, fertile soil. Height: 60–75cm; width: 30–60cm. Sun to P.M. sun.

Rose 'Morden Sunrise'

Perennial Blue Flax

Sweet Rocket
Hesperis matronalis

A clump-forming biennial that is suitable for wild gardens or a mixed border. Produces fragrant, lilac flowers in late spring to summer. Prefers fertile, moist, neutral to alkaline, well-drained soil. Height: 75–90cm; width: 30–45cm. Sun to P.M. sun.

ROSES

'Morden Sunrise' Parkland
Hardy Shrub

Striking and unusual blooms are set off against glossy foliage. Semi-double, yellow, 8–9cm flowers with orange and pink overtones bloom June through summer with a light fragrance. Height: 60–75cm; spread: 60–75cm. Sun.

Sweet Rocket

Daylily 'Raspberry Pixie'

Go ahead and try growing a few vegetables like 'Favor' carrot in a spot that doesn't get full sun all day long. Yields will be decreased but you'll still have some to harvest and enjoy fresh.

I have a small, narrow, fenced-in space running alongside my house. I want to make this unused area useful by turning it into a kitchen garden, but it doesn't get sun all day. What grows here?

Although this spot doesn't receive as much light as a traditionally located kitchen garden, you can still grow some vegetables and edible plants successfully (although they will have decreased yields). Install a raised bed filled with rich soil along the sunniest side of the space and border it with a narrow gravel path for access. In this bed you can grow edible flowers and many kinds of vegetables. Don't forget to think vertically as well, and place netting or trellis along the fence or wall for climbing vegetables to grow. Vegetables can also be grown quite successfully in large containers.

ANNUALS

Nasturtium 'Whirlybird Orange'
All parts of nasturtium are edible and are an attractive addition to salads. Semi-double, pumpkin-orange, 6cm flowers are upward facing, without spurs, and are held well above the foliage. Excellent in rock gardens, borders or as an annual groundcover. Height: 15–20cm; spacing: 15–20cm. Sun to P.M. sun.

VEGETABLES

Beans 'Straight 'n Narrow'
An outstanding, petite, deep green, French filet bean that is straight and tastes delicious. Plants are compact and 15cm pods do not overmature easily. High yields in late July to early August. Sun.

Carrot 'Favor'

These deep orange, gourmet nantes are juicy and core-less. Edible as a mini-carrot and still sweet and juicy when fully mature. Stores very well. Matures mid to late July. Sun.

Lettuce 'Bon Vivant' Leaf Mix

A beautiful mix of salad greens in a full range of colours and textures. Includes deep red, bronze and light to deep green lettuce. Can be eaten when only a few inches tall up to full size. Matures late June to early July. Seed every 14 days for continuous harvest. Sun to P.M. sun.

Lettuce 'Bon Vivant' Leaf Mix

Nasturtium 'Whirlybird Orange'

Radish 'Cheriette'

Radishes are one of the fastest crops from seed to harvest. Sow in smaller amounts several times at two-week intervals, from spring to early summer, for a continuous supply. Produces bright red, very round and tasty radishes with a mild flavour. Begin to harvest about 1 month from sowing. Sun.

Spinach 'Melody'

A hybrid variety with slightly crinkled leaves that are easy to clean. Spinach is one of the few vegetables that can be grown in partial shade. Suitable for container gardens. Produces crunchy leaves with great flavour. Begin to harvest about 1 month from sowing. P.M. sun.

Sugar Snap Pea 'Sugar Sprint'

A vine-type pea, producing tender and edible pods maturing in mid to late July. Pods are green and 7cm long. Height: 65cm. Sun.

Swiss Chard 'Bright Lights'

An edible and ornamental chard with striking cream, pink, yellow, lime and red stems and leaves. Harvest in 55 days. Sun.

Swiss Chard 'Bright Lights'

The striking blooms of bouncing bet stand out against a dark surface and help to brighten areas.

My home and fence are stained a deep chocolate-brown and my narrow side yard, consequently, feels very dark, even though this area gets four hours of sunlight in the afternoon. I want to brighten up the area by growing plants with interesting foliage, colour and texture. What grows here?

THE RANGE OF PLANTS grown for their striking foliage is vast. Choose those that will not only stand out from their surroundings, but will also work in combination. Before planting, try grouping and moving around pots of flamboyant varieties and those in deep shades of purple and green until you get the look you want. Don't choose strictly variegated foliage, as the result will be visually chaotic, and consider accessibility to the area when selecting your plants—choose varieties that won't overgrow the space or can be kept easily in check by pruning.

ANNUALS

Coleus, Wizard Series
This series provides wonderful colour in beds and containers. Available in golden, bronze and deep red shades. Height: 25–30cm; spacing: 20–25cm. Sun.

PERENNIALS

Bouncing Bet
Saponaria officinalis
Suitable for a mixed border, this drought-tolerant plant has an upright habit. Pink flowers bloom summer to fall. Thrives in fertile, well-drained soil. Height: 60–90cm; width: 60–90cm. Sun to P.M. sun.

Garden Phlox

Phlox paniculata 'David'

This award-winning variety is mildew resistant and has strong, sturdy stems and an upright habit—do not crowd. Fragrant, large, pure white flowers in mid summer. Best in moist, fertile, well-drained soil. Height: 75–100cm; width: 45–60cm. Sun to P.M. sun.

ROSES

'Morden Snow Beauty' Parkland
Hardy Shrub

Very compact, dark foliage and masses of blooms—ideal for a groundcover. Single, bright white, 9–10cm flowers bloom June to frost with a light, sweet fragrance. Height: 75–90cm; spread: 100–150cm. Sun.

TREES & SHRUBS

Dogwood 'Golden Variegated'

Cornus alba 'Gouchaltii'

Also known as 'Aureo,' this plant provides excellent contrast for large shrub beds. Produces bright green foliage with creamy-yellow edges. Height: best kept pruned to 1–2m; width: 1–1.5m. Sun to A.M. sun.

Pine 'Blue Shag'

Pinus strobus

A lovely small pine with soft and long, bluish-green needles. Excellent contrast choice for rock gardens and shrub beds. Height: 1–1.5m; width: 1.5–2m in 10–12 years. Sun.

Coleus 'Wizard Mix'

Garden Phlox 'David'

Rose 'Morden Snow Beauty'

Pine 'Blue Shag'

7
Wide-open Spaces

...nature abhors a vacuum, and so do gardeners...

I grew up on a farm with plenty of room to roam, and I loved to explore the huge trees and shrubs that grew all around us. In fact, I think growing up in that environment encouraged me to pursue the sciences, horticulture in particular. Dad loved trees too, and we planted many of them all over the farm. They have grown to maturity, and now that most of the old farm has been transformed, the trees continue to serve as windbreaks and natural park areas for new neighbourhoods.

Nature abhors a vacuum, and so do gardeners who own large yards or acreages. And therein lies the problem. The desire to fill in the vast emptiness gets many people in trouble. On the farm, for instance, because space seemed limitless, we were quick to plant but we weren't always judicious in our selections. Sometimes we didn't consider the long-term implications of our haste. As a result, innocuous spruce seedlings eventually grew to monstrous proportions. What we should have been doing was managing those wide-open spaces effectively.

A large lot, acreage or farm for that matter, that is planted just to fill the void is comparable to taking an eight-course meal, quadrupling its size and then combining all the food in a blender. The necessary ingredients are still there, but the presentation—to say nothing of the flavour—is definitely compromised. It's essential to develop pockets of interest. Try to create a series of vibrant, attractive features rather than scattering plants all over. Focus the viewer's attention rather than trying to overwhelm the senses; you want to sharpen rather than diffuse the visual impact of the plants.

To avoid creating a part- or even full-time yard-maintenance job, I recommend that you develop a realistic long-term vision and a formal plan, and then attack the job in phases. Don't be in a rush. After all, Kew Gardens wasn't created in a single season.

Creating a beautiful garden always means assessing your space, choosing the proper plants, knowing where to put them and taking a long-term view. Wide-open spaces have a lot to offer. Just be sure you don't get lost in all that vast potential. ❧

When planting in wide areas, don't forget to visually balance the space with taller selections like this 'Evans' cherry.

The sunny and wide side yard of my pie-shaped lot is bordered by a tall fence. This spot, apart from a sidewalk that leads to my back patio, is a wide expanse that I would like to enhance with all kinds of plants that will fill the area quickly. What grows here?

MOST PLANTS, INCLUDING annuals, are available in large sizes for transplanting. While these mature plants will make your side yard look well established immediately, they are more expensive than smaller specimens. If budget is a concern, consider combining a few large plants with small ones that are quick to fill in or spread. Don't overlook plants not traditionally grown in these kinds of locations, such as rhubarb or zucchini, as the rate at which they grow will offer you quick cover and an unconventional look.

ANNUALS

Castor Bean 'Green'

Useful as a fast-growing annual screen. Produces large, deeply-lobed, green foliage. Heat and drought tolerant. Height: up to 3m; spacing: 1–1.5m. Sun.

Amaranthus 'Opopeo'

Excellent in backgrounds. Dark crimson, upright flower spikes resemble a jester's cap, set off by striking bronze foliage. A warm location is a must. Height: 2–3m. Sun.

FRUIT

Cherry 'Evans'
Prunus cerasus

A very ornamental, hardy and self-pollinating cherry, producing fruit that is excellent for fresh eating, pies and winemaking. White, lightly fragrant blooms cover the branches followed by bright red, 2–3cm, sweet and tart fruit in late July or early August. Delay harvest to increase sugars. Height: 3–4m; width: 2–3m. Sun.

Castor Bean 'Green'

Amaranthus 'Opopeo'

Ribbon Grass

Lilac 'Pocohontas'

PERENNIALS

Dark Eye Sunflower
Helianthus atrorubens

Valued for its upright habit, height and
late season blooms. Deep yellow flowers
with dark red centres appear in late
summer. Prefers fertile, well-drained
soil but will tolerate dry soils. Height:
90–120cm; width: 60–90cm. Sun to
P.M. sun.

Plume Poppy
Macleaya cordata

This big, upright plant is useful as
a background or feature in a mixed
border. Large, heart-shaped, blue-grey
foliage is tropical looking. Produces
cream plumes in summer. Tolerates
some shade and prefers deep, fertile,
moist, well-drained soil. Height:
1.5–2.5m; width: 90–100cm. Sun
to P.M. sun.

Ribbon Grass
Phalaris arundinacea var. *picta*

This vigorous groundcover has interest-
ing white-striped foliage and creamy
seedheads that appear in summer.
Prefers moist, well-drained soil.
Height: 60–90cm; width: 60–90+cm.
Sun to P.M. sun.

Dark Eye Sunflower

TREES & SHRUBS

Dogwood 'Kesselring'
Cornus alba 'Kesselringii'
Dark green leaves on striking, dark brownish-purple stems. This variety is often pruned to a small tree form. Produces showy white fruit. Height: 2–2.5m; width: 2–2.5m. Sun to P.M. sun.

Elder 'Golden Plume'
Sambucus racemosa 'Plumosa Aurea'
This is a vigorous, finely textured shrub that is a super contrast plant. Bright gold foliage highlights red fruit in summer. Height: 1.5–3m; width: 1.5–3m. Sun to P.M. sun.

Lilac 'Pocohontas'
Syringa x *hyacinthiflora*
A vigorous and prolifically blooming lilac that is great for screens and shrub beds. It does not sucker. Deep violet, single blooms appear mid to late spring and are fragrant. Height: 3–4m; width: 3–4m. Sun to P.M. sun.

Maple 'Amur'
Acer tataricum ssp. *ginnala*
A beautiful feature for small yards that can be trained to a large bonsai form. Naturally it is a small, wide-spreading tree with orange-red fall colour and red, winged seeds. Produces fragrant blooms in spring. Height: 4–6m; width: 5m. Sun to P.M. sun.

Elder 'Golden Plume'

Plume Poppy

Maple 'Amur'

Combining plants with varied flowering times, along with consistently blooming annuals, will create a striking frame for a corner lot.

We have a corner lot and our side yard is wide and open to the street. We want to fill this area with plants that bloom spring through fall and really have curb appeal. What grows here?

ALTHOUGH BEDDING PLANTS will certainly provide the long-lasting colour you're looking for, don't limit yourself to just annuals. Many shrubs and perennials have colourful foliage and blooms and will add structure to your beds, providing a great background for your bright, eye-catching annuals. The foliage of decorative shrubs will also extend the effect late into the season.

ANNUALS

Sunflower 'Teddy Bear'

Very showy, bright yellow, fully double, 15cm flowers supported by strong, sturdy, branching stems. This variety makes lovely arrangements. Height: 90cm. Sun.

Petunia, Tidal Wave Series

This series is colourful and versatile—it can be grown as a spreading ground-cover or tall hedge depending on how closely you space the plants. Spacing 30cm apart results in plants growing up to 90cm. Spacing 60–75cm apart results in plants spreading to 90cm. Flowers are large and bright. Sun to P.M. sun.

PERENNIALS

Himalayan Cranesbill
Geranium himalayense

An excellent groundcover that has good fall colour. Mat-forming with violet-blue flowers early summer to fall. Prefers well-drained soil. Height: 30–45cm; width: 45–60cm. Sun to A.M. sun.

Sunflower 'Teddy Bear'

Himalayan Cranesbill

Petunia 'Tidal Wave Hot Pink'

Hydrangea 'Angel's Blush'

Ninebark 'Diabolo'

ROSES

'Nicholas' Explorer
Shrub

Produces an abundance of blooms—a great size for small shrub beds. Lightly fragrant, double, medium red, 6–7cm flowers bloom June through September. Height: 75cm; spread: 75cm. Sun.

TREES & SHRUBS

Hydrangea 'Angel's Blush'
Hydrangea paniculata 'Ruby'

A very nice accent or screen, providing blooms late into the growing season and growing larger in warmer climates. 25cm-long, white turning rosy-red, clustered flowers appear in August–September. Requires moist soil. Height: 2–3m; width: 2–3m. Sun to A.M. sun.

Lilac 'Miss Kim'
Syringa patula

A non-suckering, dwarf variety that has purple fall colour. Icy lilac-purple, very fragrant blooms open in early summer. Height: 90–150cm; width: 90–150cm. Sun to P.M. sun.

Rose 'Nicholas'

Ninebark 'Diabolo'
Physocarpus opulifolius
Great for large shrub beds or for use
as a hedge. A super contrast plant with
rich purple foliage on strong, upright
stems and pink clustered blooms in
summer. Height: 2–3m; width: 2–3m.
Sun to P.M. sun.

Spiraea 'Grefsheim'
Spiraea cinerea
Known in English as 'First Snow,' this
spiraea has white blooms smothering
the branches prior to greyish-green
foliage emerging in late May to June—
provides early impact in the season.
Use as a feature plant. Quite striking
cascading over retaining walls. Height:
1.5m; width: 1.5m. Sun.

Weigela 'Red Prince'
Weigela florida
A very nice feature in small shrub
beds and borders. Long-lasting, rich
red blooms in spring (may rebloom
in summer). Height: 1.5–2m; width:
1.5–2m. Sun.

Weigela 'Red Prince'

Lilac 'Miss Kim'

Deliberately choosing plants like 'Sutherland' elder, paying particular attention to foliage, will help create a northern version of a tropical paradise.

I love tropical plants and want to incorporate them into my large, enclosed side yard, but I don't think they'll survive the winter. This area receives direct sunlight from mid morning to mid afternoon. What grows here?

A SHELTERED, ENCLOSED AREA is the perfect summer location in which to grow many plants that have their origins in warm countries. You are correct, however, that they are not suited to harsh winter conditions. Instead, display your tropical houseplants outdoors in the summer and grow hardy plants and bulbs whose foliage and blooms have an exotic look.

PERENNIALS

Hosta
Hosta sieboldiana 'Elegans'
Hostas tolerate deep shade, but grow best in open shade with dappled sunlight. This large hosta has waxy, puckered, thick, blue-grey foliage and forms a large clump. Lavender flowers bloom in summer. Prefers moist, fertile, well-drained, organic soil. Height: 70cm; width: 150cm. Shade to A.M. sun.

Umbrella Plant
Darmera peltata
An unusual perennial—white to pink flowers emerge before foliage in early spring. Large, rounded, dark green foliage turns red in fall. Displays a low-spreading and slow-growing habit. Will tolerate dry periods, but prefers moist, boggy soil. Height: 60–90cm; width: 60–90+cm. Sun to A.M. sun.

TREES & SHRUBS

Elder 'Sutherland'
Sambucus racemosa

A fast-growing contrast shrub with lacy, golden foliage highlighting clusters of scarlet berries in July. Little pruning is required once established. Height: 2–3m; width: 2–3m. Sun to P.M. sun.

Hydrangea 'Endless Summer'
Hydrange macrophylla

An exciting introduction to northern gardens, this hardy hydrangea, hailing from Minnesota, offers 18–20cm, pink or blue, globe-shaped, clustered blooms in summer. Flower colour will be pink in alkaline soil and blue in acidic soil. Dark glossy-green foliage. Prefers moist soil. Height: 75–90cm; width: 75–90cm. A.M. to P.M. sun.

Sumac 'Staghorn'
Rhus typhina

This large shrub sports long, tropical-looking, lacy leaves on thick, velvety stems. Effective for mass planting, naturalizing, screening and at the back of shrub borders. Green blooms appear in late spring. Provides beautiful orange-red fall colour. Height: 5–7m; width: 5–7m. Sun to P.M. sun.

Willow 'Coyote'
Salix exigua

Lovely for contrast in shrub beds and a great substitute for bamboo. Feathery textured, silver-grey foliage achieves its best colour in cooler climates. Height: 2–3m; width: 2–3m. Sun to P.M. sun.

Willow 'Coyote'

Hydrangea 'Endless Summer'

Sumac 'Staghorn'

Apartment-dwelling gardeners face many challenges, but container gardening still offers a lot of choices.

I live on the eighth floor of an apartment building and would love to have a balcony garden. The balcony receives sun for six hours each day, but can be quite breezy. What grows here?

IT WON'T TAKE A LOT of plants or containers to create a full, striking, seasonal balcony garden. First, consult your building manager. Many permit residents to erect trellises or Plexiglas sheets that, when mounted in front of the railings, help to filter the wind. Following that, choose large containers filled with good-quality potting soil and consider plant supports such as obelisks, which not only help protect plants, but also offer a decorative touch. Remember, containers dry out quickly, so water often and add extra fertilizer.

ANNUALS

Celosia, Bombay Series

Very unique, 10cm, fan-shaped flowers are great in containers and mixed planters and also make good cut and dried flowers. Heat and drought tolerant. Height: 60–90cm; spacing: 30cm. Sun.

Daisy 'Snowland'

Chrysanthemum paludosum

Great in containers and short borders. Bright white, 4cm, single, daisy-like flowers on drought-tolerant plants. Height: 15cm; spacing: 15–20cm. Sun.

Lantana, Landmark Series

Although Lantana may not look like much at the bedding-out stage, it goes on to provide stunning mass displays in planters and hanging baskets. 'Pink Dawn' has rosy-pink to glowing yellow, dense, clustered flowers that attract hummingbirds. Highly fragrant foliage. Height: 35–50cm; spreads to 60cm. Sun.

Petunia, Double Wave Series

Lovely 5–8cm double flowers in wonderful colour shades easily fill hanging baskets and containers. Spreads 60–90cm. Sun.

Sweet Potato Vine 'Ace of Spades'

Ipomoea batatus

An interesting contrast plant in hanging baskets, containers, or as an annual groundcover. Displays a lush, vigorous habit with beautiful, burgundy-black, spade-shaped foliage. Height: 10–15cm; trails to 75cm. Sun to P.M. sun.

ROSES

'Flower Carpet' *Landscape*

This low-growing shrub makes an excellent groundcover and is well suited to hanging baskets and containers. Blooms are borne in clusters. Double, deep pink, 5–6cm flowers bloom from June through summer with a light fragrance. Height: 45cm; spread: 100cm. Sun.

Daisy 'Snowland'

Petunia 'Double Wave Pink'

Lantana 'Landmark Pink Dawn'

Rose 'Flower Carpet'

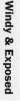

A successful rock garden incorporates a variety of interesting textures and colours that change throughout the year.

I would like to create a rock or alpine garden in our exposed and windy front yard. What grows here?

PLANTS THAT GROW NATURALLY in windy and rocky conditions can withstand the rigours of an extreme location. They may hug the ground tightly or rise just above it on strong, woody stems. Landscaped rock gardens mimic this natural environment, containing a variety of plant types, forms and sizes. They change colour constantly, with new plants blooming just as others finish, and maintain winter interest with the addition of evergreens. This type of garden improves each year as plants fill in, tumble over the rocks and self-seed in new places.

ANNUALS

Baby's Breath, Gypsy Series

Great in short borders, rock gardens and containers. Displays a profusion of dainty, tiny, single to double flowers on a plant with a fluffy, cloud-like habit. Height: 20–25cm; spacing: 35cm. Sun.

Nierembergia 'Mont Blanc'

A neat, compact plant that is drought tolerant, making it ideal in mass displays or as an annual groundcover. White, star-like, cup-shaped flowers. Mounding habit. Height: 10–15cm; spacing: 10–15cm. Sun to P.M. sun.

Sanvitalia 'Little Sun'

Masses of lemon-yellow, dark-eyed flowers on a plant with a low trailing habit. A heat and drought-tolerant choice grown as an annual groundcover or in hanging baskets. Height: 15cm; spacing: 10–15cm. Sun to P.M. sun.

PERENNIALS

Alpine Pink
Dianthus subacaulis

Suitable for a rock garden or scree bed, this mat-forming plant has evergreen foliage—do not cut back. Lovely carmine-pink to soft pink flowers bloom in summer. Requires sharply-drained soil—avoid winter wet. Height: 5–20cm; width: 15–25cm. Sun to P.M. sun.

Nierembergia 'Mont Blanc'

Sanvitalia 'Little Sun'

Alpine Woodruff
Asperula boisseri

Pretty, fragrant, pink flowers bloom in late spring on a cushion-forming ever-green plant—do not cut back. Prefers fertile, sharply-drained, gritty soil but will tolerate alkaline soils—avoid winter wet. Height 5cm; width: 10–20 cm. Sun to P.M. sun.

Creeping Speedwell
Veronica armena
'Armenian Speedwell'

A wonderful clump-forming alpine plant for the rock garden or scree bed. Rose flowers bloom in summer. Prefers sharply-drained, organic, gritty soil. Height: 5–15cm; width: 30cm. Sun to P.M. sun.

Kinnikinnik
Arctostaphylos uva-ursi

A pretty groundcover with shiny, evergreen foliage and red ornamental berries in the fall. White to soft pink flowers appear in spring. Drought

tolerant once established but prefers moist, well-drained, acidic, fertile soil. Height: 10–15cm; width: 45–60cm. Sun to P.M. sun.

Nipple Cactus
Coryphantha missouriensis

Grow this cactus in a hot and dry, sheltered location. Yellow-green or pink flowers appear in early summer followed by red-tinted green fruits in fall. Thrives in organic, sharply-drained, gritty soil. Height: 4–5cm; width: 10–15cm. Sun.

Prickly Thrift
Acantholimon bracteatum
ssp. *capitatum*

Prickly, evergreen foliage on a cushion form and striking flower spikes make this plant a real conversation piece. Bright pink flowers bloom in summer. This slow-growing perennial resents being moved. Requires sharply-drained, alkaline, dry soil—avoid winter wet and do not cut back. Height: 10–15 cm; width: 15–25 cm. Sun.

Nipple Cactus

Alpine Woodruff

Creeping Speedwell

Spiral Bellflower
Campanula cochlearifolia
'R.B. Loder'

A resilient plant, tuft-forming and creeping in habit, it grows in scree beds, rock gardens, crevices and along pathways. Produces blue flowers in summer. Prefers moist, well-drained, gritty soil. Height: 10–15cm; width: 45–60cm. Sun to P.M. sun.

Spring Adonis
Adonis vernalis

Very attractive yellow flowers resembling buttercups bloom atop mounding, fern-like foliage in early spring. Dislikes being disturbed. Prefers fertile, well-drained, alkaline soil. Height: 15–30cm; width: 20–30cm. Sun to P.M. sun.

TREES & SHRUBS

Spiraea 'Dakota Goldcharm'
Spiraea japonica 'Mertyann'

A short accent plant that provides contrast in borders, shrub beds and rock gardens. Yellow to bronze-tipped branches highlight bright pink blooms in mid June. Remove spent flowers to promote reblooming. Height: 30–40cm; width: 60–90cm. Sun.

Juniper 'Alpine Carpet'
Juniperus communis 'Mondap'

A great choice for areas with limited space. Soft-textured, deep blue-green foliage on a hardy, slow-growing groundcover that looks lovely against rock. Height: 20–25cm; width: 90–100cm. Sun.

Spruce 'Mrs. Cesarini'
Picea pungens

A showy, nest-like spruce for rock gardens or small shrub beds. Rich brown buds open to pale green foliage that stands out against older needles. Height: 75–90cm; width: 100–150cm in 15 years. Sun.

Spruce 'Mrs. Cesarini'

Spiral Bellflower 'R.B. Loder'

Spring Adonis

Windy & Exposed

'Compact Blue' spruce and 'Bailey Select Schubert' chokecherry can create an urban-scale windbreak and still allow a view.

We live on the edge of a school field and are interested in screening the wind and snow that comes off it. What grows here?

I T IS DIFFICULT TO CREATE a full-size windbreak on an urban lot because of space constraints. There are some smaller trees and evergreens, however, which are worth considering for this purpose. Be aware that you will be altering your view and making your yard feel much more enclosed. Another option is a tall and deep border made of dense shrubs, tall perennials and bright annuals, which will provide relief from the elements, allow an open feeling and still maintain some of your view.

PERENNIALS

Aster
Aster novi-belgii 'Patricia Ballard'

Suitable for any mixed border, this clump-forming plant has lavender-pink flowers in late summer to fall. Avoid overcrowding and always water at its base. Prefers fertile, well-drained, moist soil. Height: 60–75 cm; width: 30–45 cm. Sun to P.M. sun.

Daylily
Hemerocallis 'Flasher'

Grass-like, clump-forming foliage holds up well to wind. Bright tangerine flowers appear in mid July to early August. Prefers moist, fertile, well-drained soil. Height: 60cm; width: 45–75cm. Sun to P.M. sun.

Western Sage
Artemisia ludoviciana 'SilverKing'

Thriving in a hot and dry location, this clump-forming perennial displays silver-grey foliage, which can be used in flower arrangements. Prune back hard in spring. Does best in well-drained, alkaline, poor, dry soil. Height: 60–90cm; width: 60–90+cm. Sun.

TREES & SHRUBS

Buffaloberry 'Silver'
Shepherdia argentea

A native plant of Alberta. Although often thought of for stabilizing hillsides, it makes an effective naturalizing screen. Silver-grey foliage is displayed on young silver branches that turn brown with age. Bright orange fruit in the fall. Great for hot, dry sites. Height: 2–5m; width: 2–5m. Sun.

Aster 'Patricia Ballard'

Western Sage 'SilverKing'

Juniper 'Cologreen'

Honeysuckle 'Honeyrose'
Lonicera

Great for screens, backgrounds or features. Deep bluish-green foliage with rosy-red spring blooms. Resistant to Witch's Broom aphid. Height: 3m; width: 2–3m. Sun to P.M. sun.

Juniper 'Cologreen'
Juniperus scopulorum

Plant Cologreen in a row for an attractive, dense screen. Great for rock gardens and small yards. Requires little shearing or pruning. A beautiful, upright, cone-like form. Height: 5–6m; width: 1.5–2m. Sun to P.M. sun.

Juniper 'Moonglow'
Juniperus scopulorum

Intense bluish-grey foliage on a dense, pyramidal form that makes a great feature or screen. Considered a fast-growing evergreen that is very attractive planted in groups. Requires no shearing or pruning. Height: 6m; width: 1.5m. Sun.

Buffaloberry 'Silver'

Chokecherry
'Bailey Select Schubert'
Prunus virginiana

A colourful feature tree—excellent for small yards. This small, fast-growing, round-headed form of chokecherry has pretty, clustered, white blooms in spring, followed by edible black fruit. Green leaves turn a deep reddish-purple in early summer and have a lovely purple fall colour. Height: 6–7m; width: 5–6m. Sun.

Spruce 'Compact Blue'
Picea pungens 'Compacta'

Just the right height and spread for a small yard—makes a great feature or background. Provides stunning contrast with its intense cool blue colour. Height: 3–4m; width: 2–3m in 15 years. Sun to P.M. sun.

Variegated Wayfaring Tree
Viburnum lantana 'Varigatum'

A very showy contrast shrub—great for backgrounds. Random variegation of dark green, light green and creamy white leaves—no two leaves are the same. Showy white blooms in spring followed by bright red berries in fall. Height: 2–3m; width: 2–3m. Sun.

Variegated Wayfaring Tree

Juniper 'Moonglow'

8

Specifically
Speaking

...the result has been
well worth the effort...

We've all fought with those truly inhospitable areas of the garden, the incredibly hot or super wet areas that seem to be the kiss of death to even the toughest plants. It seems that no matter what you try to grow there, the plants either burn out from lack of sunlight or burn up from too much.

When confronting this "No Plant's Land," gardeners may act in desperation, following the classic fight-or-flight strategy. Some fight the lack of light in heavily shaded spots and try every imaginable species, seemingly at random, desperately hoping that one will take hold. Others, confronted by sun-bleached zones of destruction, simply surrender to what they think is the inevitable and put down gravel.

Rather than waste time and money on the shotgun approach or just give up, I've tried to work with so-called impossible spots by researching and choosing the right plants and then, when I can, modifying the environment to make it a little more hospitable.

Take, for example, this common problem: a hot, dry, southwest-facing slope. Spots like this, which take the full brunt of the sun's rays, can be many degrees warmer than other areas in your yard. The best way to handle this spot is to start with the soil. Adding lots of rich organic matter will help the soil hold more moisture and reduce the stress on plants. Add drought-tolerant species, and you've gone a long way to eliminating the problem.

Working with the environment usually means just that: working. When I purchased my current home a few years ago, it came with large spruce trees. They were too big for the site and dropped needles all over the place. I could have ignored the problem or fought with the trees, but instead chose to remove them. After the spruce was gone, the acidic soil would have required a major overhaul to grow anything successfully and I wasn't looking to add a new bed. So I installed a patio and put large planters on it. In the summer, the planters play host to whichever annuals strike my fancy; in the winter, I put in evergreen arrangements for the holiday season.

Does that sound like a lot of work and money to solve a problem? Well, maybe it was. But to me, the result has been well worth the effort, and the expense was less than season after season of unsuccessful trial and error. There are many ways to address even the most intractable spots in the yard. A change in perspective combined with a little creativity can yield a solution without exhausting your resources. ❧

'Cutleaf Weeping' birch thrives in a moist, sunny yard, rewarding us with a cascading form and golden fall colours.

We have the lowest front yard on our block and although it is sunny, it seldom dries out. We would like to add a variety of plants, including trees and shrubs. What grows here?

ALTHOUGH SOME MIGHT view this type of location as a problem, most gardeners would give their eye teeth for sun and consistent moisture! Avoid using any plants that dislike having wet feet and avoid the temptation to water the garden indiscriminately; check the soil for moisture and then water only when necessary.

ANNUALS

Castor Bean 'Red'
Ricinus communis 'Sanguineus'
Useful as a fast-growing annual screen. Large, reddish-green, deeply-lobed foliage. Heat and drought tolerant. Height: up to 3m; spacing: 1–1.5m. Sun.

PERENNIALS

Blue Flag Iris
Iris versicolor
Makes a wonderful water garden plant or can be used in any border if kept moist. Clump forming with light blue flowers in late spring. Prefers alkaline-free, wet, organic soil. Height: 20–80cm; width: 45–60cm. Sun to A.M. sun.

Creeping Jenny
Lysimachia nummularia

Use as a groundcover even in wet areas, on slopes and in lean soil. Roots where it creeps and touches the soil. Golden yellow flowers appear in late spring to summer on foliage that remains evergreen. Prefers organic, moist well-drained soil. Height: 2–5cm; width 45–60+cm. Sun or shade.

TREES & SHRUBS

Birch 'Cutleaf Weeping'
Betula pendula 'Lacinata'

A very graceful weeping form with deeply cut leaves that create a fine textured look on long, arching branches reaching to the ground. The bark is a beautiful bright white. Produces catkins in the spring. Thrives in moist locations. Height: 15m; width: 6–10m. Sun.

Bog Rosemary 'Blue Ice'
Andromeda polifolia

Also known as 'Andromeda,' this plant provides nice contrast in mixed evergreen beds. Dusty blue foliage on a hardy, dense, compact form. Keep it compact by shearing and shaping when actively growing. Requires moist or wet soil. Height: 30–45cm; width: 60–90cm. Sun to P.M. sun.

Hydrangea 'Lime Light'
Hydrangea paniculata

Attractive flowerheads held straight up are great for large shrub beds. Bright green blooms in mid to late summer are excellent for drying. Requires moist, well-drained soil. Height: 2–3m; width: 1.5–2m. Sun to P.M. sun.

Mayday 'Advance'
Prunus padus

Mature trees have attractive, dark, steel-grey bark. This extremely hardy variety originated in southern Alberta and is stunning when in full bloom (usually a week ahead of the species). Produces white, clustered, sweetly-scented flowers. A tall columnar form, that suits small yards. Height: 9–12m; width: 3–3.5m. Sun.

Creeping Jenny

Hydrangea 'Lime Light'

Blue Flag Iris

Soften the look of rock mulch by incorporating different forms of plants and varying the size of the stones.

We've just moved into a home where the previous owners mulched the sunny front beds in rock. We would like to add some plants, without removing all of the gravel. What grows here?

PLANTS USED IN XERISCAPING (low-water design) tend to look appropriate among gravel beds. The key is to place the plants near to each other in groupings of three or more. Otherwise, the plants appear to be lost in a sea of rock. As well, use plants of differing heights and form to create a more natural appearance. You also have the simplest option of grouping containers of plants in a pleasing arrangement on top of the gravel.

ANNUALS

Portulaca, Yubi Series

Vigorous plants that trail to 45cm—ideal in containers and rock gardens and is also a superb groundcover. Low maintenance and very floriferous. Produces vibrantly coloured, 6cm, single flowers. Prominent stamens and centres are very attractive. Outstanding heat, drought and wind tolerance. Height: 7–15cm. Sun.

PERENNIALS

Achillea
Achillea millefolium 'Paprika'

Very heat and drought tolerant with cherry-red, yellow-centred flowers that will stand out against the gravel. Blooms early summer to fall, and has an upright habit. Height: 30-60cm; width: 45–60+cm. Sun to P.M. sun.

Adam's Needle
Yucca filamentosa

Valued for its bold upright form. Produces dark green, spiky evergreen foliage edged with curly, white thread—do not cut back. White flowers tinged yellow bloom in summer. Does best in a sheltered site away from cold, drying winds. Well-drained soil—avoid winter wet. Height: 60–75cm; width: 60–100cm. Sun.

Alpine Poppy
Papaver alpinum

A tuft-forming plant with grey-green foliage and attractive yellow, orange, pink or white flowers blooming spring and most of summer. Requires sharply-drained soil. Height: 15cm; width: 15cm. Sun to P.M. sun.

Hot & Dry

Achillea 'Paprika'

Alpine Poppy

Adam's Needle

Portulaca 'Yubi Yellow'

Fleabane
Erigeron

Pink daisy-like flowers resemble asters but bloom earlier and make a good cutflower. Flowers in summer and is clump-forming (may require staking). Prefers sharply-drained, fertile, moist soil. Height: 45cm; width 45cm. Sun to P.M. sun.

TREES & SHRUBS

Juniper 'Hughes'
Juniperus horizontalis

An excellent juniper for rock gardens or large shrub beds and often grown as a thick groundcover. 'Hughes' displays compact silvery-blue foliage. Height: 45–50cm; width: 1–1.5m. Sun to P.M. sun.

Potentilla 'Yellowbird'

Pine 'Tannenbaum'
Pinus mugo

A very hardy and drought-tolerant pine with a pyramidal form. Produces dark green, very dense foliage from top to bottom. A beautiful dwarf Christmas tree. Height: 4m; width: 2m. Sun to P.M. sun.

Potentilla 'Yellowbird'
Potentilla fruticosa

An upright form with bright yellow, semi-double blooms in summer. Great for hedging, borders or as a feature in a shrub bed. Thrives in a hot dry site. Height: 90cm; width: 90cm. Sun.

Spruce 'Nest'
Picea abies 'Nidiformis'

Great in shrub beds and borders. Usually has a slight depression on the top that makes it look like a nest. New growth contrasts with older dark green needles on a flat-topped, bun-shaped form. Height: 1m; width: 1.5m in 15–20 years. Sun to P.M. sun.

Spruce 'Nest'

Fleabane

Juniper 'Hughes'

'Vancouver Gold' genista stands up to hot conditions and puts on a spectacular show of colour each spring.

We have a sunny, front courtyard that gets brutally hot by midday. What grows here?

TAKE A CUE FROM Mediterranean courtyards of old and choose heat and drought-tolerant plants grown in interesting containers or in the ground if the area is not completely paved. Plants with strong architectural forms are welcome additions to structured spaces as opposed to floppier, more casual cottage plants. Courtyards tend to house microclimates, so experiment with plants that are borderline hardy in a more open space.

ANNUALS

Salvia, Victoria Series
Salvia farinacea
Narrow spikes of silvery-white and deep violet-blue florets highlight this series, which is a good substitute for lavender. Attracts hummingbirds and makes a good cut or dried flower. Height: 30–35cm. Sun.

Poppy 'Thai Silk Rose Chiffon'
This California-type poppy has finely cut, grey-green foliage that supports golden-centred, soft rose, 7cm, semi-double flowers. Excellent heat and drought tolerance. Height: 25cm. Sun.

PERENNIALS

Globe Centaurea
Centaurea macrocephala

Large, fuzzy, thistle-like, yellow flowers bloom late spring to late summer
atop clump-forming foliage. Drought
tolerant but prefers moist, fertile, well-
drained soil. Height: 90–100cm; width:
90–100cm. Sun to P.M. sun.

Russian Sage
Perovskia atriplicifolia

Suitable for hot, dry sites and lovely
combined with brightly coloured
perennials. Aromatic, grey foliage is
upright and sub-shrubby in habit.
Blue-mauve flowers appear in late
summer and dry well. Prefers poor
to moderately fertile, well-drained
soil and is tolerant of dry and alkaline soil. Height: 75–100cm; width:
60–90cm. Sun.

Small Globe Thistle
Echinops ritro

A heat and drought-tolerant addition
to a border or wild garden. Silver-grey
foliage is clump forming and compact
in habit. Blue flowers appearing in late
summer attract butterflies and are excellent for cutting and drying. Thrives in
poor, well-drained soil. Height: 60cm;
width: 45cm. Sun to P.M. sun.

TREES & SHRUBS

Genista 'Vancouver Gold'
Genista pilosa

Hundreds of yellow blooms cover this
heat-loving groundcover in spring—
extremely showy. Great for mass planting and rock gardens. Height: 30cm;
width: 90–100cm. Sun.

Harry Lauder's Walkingstick
Corylus avellana 'Contorta'

An interesting feature shrub that is
trainable to a small tree. Displays showy
spring catkins and unique curled
branches and leaves. Remove any
shoots originating below ground as
these take over the plant and destroy
its unique growth habit. Plant in a
wind-protected site. Height: 1.5–3m;
width: 1.5–3m. Sun to P.M. sun.

Globe Centaurea

Harry Lauder's Walkingstick

Russian Sage

Fuss-free cherry prinsepia is an excellent choice for use in gardens that receive little attention.

The front of our cottage is somewhat shady and receives very little attention most of the year. We would like to plant some shrubs or perennials that will thrive on neglect. What grows here?

PLANTS NATIVE TO the woods around your cottage will be indicators of what survives in this location. One option is to choose from cultivated varieties of these plants sold at your local nursery. Bear in mind that wildlife may browse on your plants, so protect accordingly. Remember, in order for your plants to establish well, in the first and, perhaps, second season, they will require some initial attention.

PERENNIALS

Longleaf Lungwort
Pulmonaria 'Cotton Cool'
A very tough plant for use as a ground-cover for a woodland or border edging. Clump-forming in habit with narrow, silvery foliage and blue flowers in spring. Thrives in fertile, well-drained, organic soil. Height: 20–30cm; width 45–60cm. Shade to A.M. sun.

Garden Globeflower
Trollius x *cultorum*
Perfect for moist, woodland gardens, pond sides or shady borders providing globe-shaped, orange flowers in spring to mid summer. Clump-forming in habit—cut back after flowering for more blooms. Prefers moist, fertile soil. Height: 60–90cm; width 45cm. Shade to A.M. sun.

ROSES

'Hansa' *Hybrid Rugosa*

One of the best all-round hardy shrub rugosas—very long-lived, dense in form and hardy to Zone 1. Double, fuchsia-red, 8–10cm flowers have a strong clove-like fragrance. Blooms heavily in June or July and repeats all summer. Height: 1.5–2m; spread: 1.5–2m. Sun.

'Red Rugosa' *Hybrid Rugosa*

This hardy shrub rose is resistant to black spot and powdery mildew. Pretty blooms are followed by large red rose-hips. Single, blue-red, 10cm flowers bloom in June and sporadically through summer, with a moderate fragrance. Height: 1.5–2m; spread: 1.5–2m. Sun.

TREES & SHRUBS

Cherry Prinsepia
Prinsepia sinensis

This landscape plant produces edible fruit in August. Good for hedges and as a fuss-free foundation plant. Height: 2–3m; width: 2-3m. Sun.

Cranberry 'Alfredo Compact'
Viburnum trilobum

An extremely compact plant with very dense foliage and striking red fall colour—ideal for hedging or borders. Produces bright red, edible fruits. Height: 1.5–2m; width: 1.5–2m. Sun to P.M. sun.

Dogwood 'Siberian Pearls'
Cornus alba

Dark green foliage and masses of pearly-white berries highlight this pretty shrub. Rich reddish-purple colour in fall. Deep red stems provide winter interest. Height: 2–3m; width: 2–3m. Sun to P.M. sun.

Dogwood 'Siberian Pearls'

Garden Globeflower

Rose 'Hansa'

Rose 'Red Rugosa'

Shady

The foliage of Bethlehem sage makes an attractive border in shady areas.

Our neighbours have covered their part of our shared side yard with landscape fabric and bright white rock. Although the rock serves to lighten this shaded area, the sheer volume of it is quite overwhelming. We would like to plant something, perhaps shrubs, in the slender, 30cm section of soil running between their rock and our sidewalk. What grows here?

PART OF LIVING AS closely as we do in urban settings is learning how to work with our neighbours' design preferences. Your very narrow strip is limiting as far as choosing shrubs, but there are quite a few perennials and annuals well suited to the site. If the soil in this area seldom dries out, choose shade-tolerant, moisture-loving plants. Single-selection, mass plantings will make the space appear long and formal, while mixed plantings will visually shorten and soften the space.

ANNUALS

Begonia 'Pin-up Flame'

An award-winning tuberous variety displaying red-edged, golden-peach, very large, single flowers. Excellent in hanging baskets, containers and beds. Height: 20–25cm; spacing: 15–25cm. Shade to A.M. sun.

Perilla 'Magilla'

A superb contrast plant that is ideal in mixed planters and garden beds. Burgundy-edged leaves with red and green highlights are very attractive. Heat tolerant. Height: up to 45cm; spacing: 20cm. Sun or shade.

PERENNIALS

Auricula Primrose
Primula auricula

A very hardy primrose for northern climes. Fragrant blooms appear in spring and are available in mixed colours. Clump forming in habit—do not cut back. Requires moist, well-drained, organic, soil—avoid winter wet. Height: 15–25cm; width: 20–30cm. Shade to A.M. sun.

Bethlehem Sage
Pulmonaria saccharata

Very tough plants for use as a groundcover for a woodland or border edging. Clump-forming, spotted foliage with rose-red, opening to blue, flowers in spring. Prefers fertile, well-drained, organic soil. Height: 20–30cm; width: 45–60cm. Shade to A.M. sun.

Creeping Phlox
Phlox stolonifera 'Blue Ridge'

Great for use in woodland gardens, borders or shady rock gardens. A mat-forming, spreading plant with evergreen foliage and blue flowers in late

spring to summer. Prefers well-drained, moist, fertile, neutral to acidic soil. Height: 15–25cm; width: 30–45+cm. Shade to A.M. sun.

Hosta
Hosta 'Red October'

Hostas tolerate deep shade, but grow best in open shade with dappled sunlight. This smaller hosta has green foliage and prominent red stems. Clump forming. Lavender flowers bloom in summer. Prefers moist, fertile, well-drained, organic soil. Height: 20–30cm; width: 45–60cm. Shade to A.M. sun.

Variegated Heartleaf Forget-Me-Not
Brunnera macrophylla 'Hadspen Cream'

Use as a groundcover in a woodland site or in a shady border. A colony-forming plant with heart-shaped, variegated foliage and blue flowers in spring. Thrives in moist, well-drained, fertile, organic soil. Height: 30–40cm; width: 35–40cm. Shade to A.M. sun.

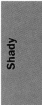

Shady

Perilla 'Magilla'

Hosta 'Red October'

Begonia 'Pin-Up Flame'

Containers filled with shade-tolerant annuals are a simple way of dealing with tree roots.

We have a large, open-headed tree that casts dappled shade over most of our front yard. The roots are somewhat exposed, and the lawn doesn't do well around them. We're more than willing to try an alternative to grass. What grows here?

IN THE MOISTURE BATTLE between healthy, lush lawns and large trees, the tree almost always wins. There are many solutions other than grass, however, to deal with your moisture and light issues. Grow drought- and shade-tolerant plants beneath the tree's canopy or consider applying attractive bark mulch and grouping planters filled with colourful annuals.

ANNUALS

Lobelia, Regatta Series
Masses of tiny, fragrant flowers make lobelia a great choice for baskets and containers. Regatta is available in shades of lilac, blue and white. Mounds and trails to 25cm. A.M. or P.M. sun.

Impatiens, Dazzler Series
A reliable bloomer for shaded hanging baskets, containers and flowerbeds. The Dazzler series is available in a range of individual colours and blends. Produces masses of distinctive, 4cm, single flowers. Height: 20–25cm; spacing: 10–15cm. Shade to A.M. sun.

PERENNIALS

Heartleaf Bergenia
Bergenia 'Perfect'

A very versatile plant and slightly taller than most varieties. Grows in a wide range of soils and moisture conditions. Clump-forming, evergreen foliage spreads more rapidly in moist soils. Do not cut back in fall. Rose-red flowers bloom in spring. Height: 40–45cm; width: 45–60cm. Sun or shade.

Himalayan Fleece Flower
Persicaria affinis 'Darjeeling Red'

A long-blooming evergreen ground-cover that produces spikes of pink flowers aging to burnt red, mid summer to fall. Good for dried arrangements. Grows in a moist or dry area but prefers moist, fertile soil. Height: 15–25cm; width: 60–90+cm. Sun to A.M. sun.

Mountain Bluet
Centaurea montana

A clump-forming plant that produces star-shaped, deep blue blooms in late-spring to late summer—excellent cutflowers. Although drought tolerant, it prefers moist, fertile, well-drained soil. Will self-seed. Height: 60–90cm; width: 60–90cm. Sun to A.M. sun.

TREES & SHRUBS

Juniper 'Calgary Carpet'
Juniperus sabina 'Monna'

An extremely popular juniper that is tolerant of light shade. Very soft green foliage on a low-growing, spreading shrub. Prefers dry soil. Height: 20–30cm; width: 2–3m. Sun to P.M. sun.

Oregon Grapeholly
Mahonia aquifolium

A slow-growing shrub often used in rock gardens or shrub beds. Shiny, dark green foliage highlights blue-black fruit and turns purplish-red in fall. Height: 1–2m; width: 1–1.5m. Shade to A.M. sun.

Impatiens 'Dazzler Red'

Himalayan Fleece Flower 'Darjeeling Red'

Lobelia 'Regatta Sapphire'

Mountain Bluet

'Dwarf' genista roots tenaciously, anchoring soil and providing a long season of blooms.

Our yard slopes downward from the front street to a man-made lake behind our backyard. The soil surrounding our home is bare and erosion is a real problem every time it rains. What grows here?

COVERING THE SOIL is the easiest means of stopping the loss of valuable topsoil. Plants that effectively control erosion typically have branches that root where they touch the earth or roots that aggressively spread underground. Any plant, however, will help to anchor the soil. The most popular and appropriate landscape solution is to install terraces or a retaining wall system that slows run-off and provides interesting level pockets in which to plant.

ANNUALS

Petunia, Wave Series
Excellent in hanging baskets and containers, or as an annual groundcover. Covered in 5–7cm flowers in a wide variety of colours. A very vigorous, flat growth habit. Weather tolerant. Height: 15cm; spreads to 120cm. Sun to P.M. sun.

PERENNIALS

Himalayan Fleece Flower
Persicaria affinis
A long-blooming evergreen groundcover that produces spikes of pink flowers aging to burnt red, mid summer to fall. Good for dried arrangements. Grows in a moist or dry area but prefers moist, fertile soil. Height: 15–25cm; width: 60–90+cm. Sun to A.M. sun.

Cliff Green

Paxistima canbya

This plant has a spreading habit with foliage that remains evergreen and produces green-white flowers in summer. Prefers organic, moist, well-drained, neutral to acidic soil. Height: 20–40cm; width: 45–60cm. Sun or shade.

Snow-in-Summer

Cerastium tomentosum

A great groundcover for poor soils and dry slopes. Woolly, grey foliage is mat-forming. Displays white flowers in late spring to early summer. Prefers dry, well-drained soil. Height: 15–20cm; width: 90–100+cm. Sun.

TREES & SHRUBS

Genista 'Dwarf'

Genista lydia

Abundant yellow blooms last 3–5 weeks on this excellent groundcover plant. Great for hot dry areas. Height: 45–60cm; width: 90–100cm. Sun.

Juniper 'Calgary Carpet'

Juniperus sabina 'Monna'

An extremely popular juniper that is tolerant of light shade. Very soft green foliage on a low-growing, spreading shrub. Prefers dry soil. Height: 20–30cm; width: 2–3m. Sun.

Stephanandra 'Cutleaf'

Stephanandra incisa 'Crispa'

A fine-textured, compact groundcover with reddish-bronze new foliage and reddish-orange fall colour. Lovely spilling over rocks, rooting where its branches touch the soil—great on slopes. Height: 30–60cm; width: 1–2m. Sun to P.M. sun.

Sumac 'Gro-Low'

Rhus aromatica

Excellent for massing in beds or for erosion control. Compact, aromatic foliage displays yellow, scented blooms in late spring. Nice red fall colour. Height: 2–3m; width: 2–3m. Sun.

Slopes

Juniper 'Calgary Carpet'

Stephanandra 'Cutleaf'

Petunia 'Wave Purple'

When you create a view, consider all sides of your proposed planting, both looking out from your home and into your yard from the street.

The front view from our home is very unattractive and uninspiring. We would like to enhance it, perhaps planting along the front property line, but not obscure our house from the street. What grows here?

CONSIDER THE SITUATION carefully, and create a screen for the most undesirable aspect. Depending on the situation, a single, open-headed tree, a hedge or a line of trees staggered in height may block out the bad view, but not your house. A clustered planting of varying heights may be enough to direct the eye away from the unpleasant view, especially if you use colourful plants and extra features such as statuary and large rocks.

PERENNIALS

Double Queen of the Meadow
Filipendula ulmaria 'Flore Pleno'

A clump-forming plant with fragrant, double, creamy-white flowers in early summer. Thrives in a boggy site and will tolerate more sun if kept moist. Prefers well-drained, moist, organic soil. Height: 60–90cm; width: 60cm. Shade to A.M. sun.

Black-Eyed Susan
Rudbeckia fulgida var. *sullivantii* 'Goldsturm'

Produces masses of deep yellow, daisy-like flowers with dark brown centres all summer and into fall. Great for cutflowers. Drought tolerant and grows well in poor soil but prefers moist, well-drained and fertile soil. Height: 45–60cm; width: 30–45cm. Sun.

TREES & SHRUBS

Aspen 'Swedish Columnar'
Populus tremula 'Erecta'

Beautiful planted in groups as a screen or windbreak—good for small yards or tight spaces. This tree has shallow non-invasive roots. Small round leaves tremble at the slightest breeze on a tall, hardy columnar form. Height: 10m; width: 1.5–2m. Sun.

Black-Eyed Susan 'Goldsturm'

Juniper 'Tolleson's Weeping'

Aspen 'Swedish Columnar'

Creating a View

Pincherry 'Jumping Pound'

Cherry 'Jumping Pound Pincherry'
Prunus pensylvanica

A small ornamental tree with great fall colour. Produces 10–12mm, bright red fruit in August to September that is good for juice, syrup and wine. Height: 7–10m; width: 6–7m. Sun.

Hawthorn 'Toba'
Crataegus x *mordenensis*

Great for small yards, screens or near decks as it produces no thorns or fruit. Light pink, fragrant, double blooms appear in spring. Height: 6m; width: 6m. Sun to P.M. sun.

Juniper 'Tolleson's Weeping'
Juniperus scopulorum

A striking feature plant that ages to its best form. Silver-blue foliage hangs mane-like from long arching branches—dramatic. Height: 5–7m; width: 2–3m. Sun.

Hawthorn 'Toba'

Cranberry 'Wentworth'
Viburnum trilobum

This lovely shrub makes an attractive screen. Clustered creamy-white blooms in spring are followed by heavy yields of bright red, edible berries that are good for juices and jellies. Displays intense fall colour. Height: 3–4m; width: 3–4m. Sun to P.M. sun.

Ornamental Crabapple 'Big River'
Malus

A very showy, pyramidal tree with great scale and fireblight resistance. Perfect tree for the smaller yard. 2–3cm, deep rose-pink, lightly fragrant blooms appear in May. Height: 6–7m; width: 2–3m. Sun.

Pine 'Scotch'
Oriental Pompon Form
Pinus sylvestris

The branches of this Scotch pine are trained to form cloud-like structures of foliage, making a custom feature in Japanese or large rock gardens. Height and width are training dependent. Sun.

Spruce 'Iseli Columnar Blue'
Picea pungens 'Iseli Fastigiate'

Excellent for small yards. Striking flanking a driveway or house entrance. Compact, steel blue foliage on a very narrow, upright form. Height: 10–20m; width: 3–4m. Sun.

Spruce 'Iseli Columnar Blue'

Pine 'Scotch'—Oriental Pompon Form

9
Art
in the Garden

...one piece set the tone...

Art in the garden is as varied as the personalities of those who choose to display it. It can be lighthearted, like the garden flamingo or gnome, or it can evoke strong memories, like the rusty old horse-drawn plough my father put in his garden. Being a farmer, for Dad the plough represented the struggles of the early pioneers who transformed the prairie into what we see today. That one piece set the tone for his entire garden.

Some gardeners take a more pragmatic approach, making function as important as form. They might choose useful accessories such as benches, obelisks or birdbaths rather than purely evocative pieces like Dad's plough. Other people don't add art to their gardens at all, perhaps because they want to keep the look as natural as possible, or perhaps because they simply don't want to bother—more often the latter, I suspect. But art is present in one form or another anyway, whether it's in the graceful curve of a felled branch or in the stones you piled in the corner.

I take after my father. I like a decorative touch, provided it's tasteful and suits the yard's overall look. In the large stone planters on my front patio, I've used tall iron pyramids that terminate in decorative finials as a striking and dramatic framework for climbing vines. And I've specifically chosen decorative finishes for some of my permanent features, such as the stone that faces my raised beds. I like containers and have learned that a few decorative pots will go a long way to changing the feel of my yard.

Of course, some people like garden gnomes and pink flamingos, and I'm not about to argue with them. Beauty is, after all, in the eye of the beholder. Sometimes you put on a show for others, and sometimes it's just for yourself. ✢

A well-placed birdbath provides a visual feature and welcomes visitors to your garden.

I received a lovely birdbath as a gift. I'd like to place it in a somewhat shady part of my yard and enclose it with plants. What grows here?

SURROUNDING A BIRDBATH with plants creates a very welcoming and sheltered spot for birds. Most birdbaths stand about 60–90cm tall; place taller plants behind the piece with progressively shorter plants to the sides and front. This will allow you to easily access the bath for cleaning and filling. It will also make the bath a visual feature in this shady area of your garden, especially if you use plants that have variegated foliage or light-coloured blooms.

Annuals

Begonia, Non-Stop Series

Bright, clear colours and stunning, large, double flowers make this series a winner. Height: 20–25cm; spacing: 15–25cm. Shade to A.M. sun.

Perennials

Foam Flower
Tiarella cordifolia 'Mint Chocolate'

Grow as a groundcover in a shady border or woodland garden. Pink-tinted flowers bloom in spring above clump-forming, mint-green and chocolate foliage. Tolerates most soils but prefers moist, organic, acidic soil—avoid winter wet; cool site. Height: 20–40cm; width: 30cm. Shade to A.M. sun.

American Alumroot
Heuchera americana (Dale's strain)

Silver-mottled foliage on a great groundcover. Tiny, greenish-white flowers bloom on stalks in early summer. Replant every two years in fall as crowns tend to push upwards. Thrives in moist, fertile, well-drained soil. Height: 60–75cm; width: 25–30cm. Shade to A.M. sun.

Begonia 'Non-Stop Apricot'

Browallia 'Blue Bells'

Foam Flower 'Mint Chocolate'

Circle Flower 'Alexander'

Circle Flower
Lysimachia punctata 'Alexander'

An upright and spreading plant that grows best in damp borders, wood-land gardens and along pond margins. White and green variegated foliage highlights gold flowers in mid to late summer. Thrives in organic, moist, well-drained soil. Height: 50–75cm; width: 45–60+cm. Sun to P.M. sun.

Goldleaf Bleeding Heart
Dicentra spectabilis 'Goldheart'

A clump-forming plant with lime-green foliage and pink flowers in spring to early summer. Use as a groundcover in a woodland garden—avoid hot, windy sites. Best in moist, well-drained, fertile, organic soil. Height: 75–90cm; width: 75–90cm. Shade to A.M. sun.

Japanese Painted Fern
Athyrium niponicum var. *pictum* 'Silver Falls'

Suitable for a shady border. Silvery foliage with red veins on a creeping, upright fern. Requires moist, fertile, neutral to acidic, organic soil. Height: 40cm; width: 30cm. Shade to A.M. sun.

Goldleaf Bleeding Heart 'Goldheart'

TREES & SHRUBS

Dogwood 'Ivory Halo'
Cornus alba 'Bailhalo'

A very nice contrast or accent shrub
with compact, silver variegated foliage.
Vivid red twigs are striking in winter.
A very compact and slow-growing
variety requiring little pruning.
Prefers moist soil. Height: 1.5–2m;
width: 1.5–2m. Sun to P.M. sun.

Hydrangea 'Kyushu'
Hydrangea paniculata

A lovely feature shrub with smooth,
dark green leaves and abundant white
blooms that fade to pink. Blooms in-
shade but requires some direct sun to
reach its full potential. Requires moist
soil. Height: 2–3m; width: 2–3m. Sun
to P.M. sun.

Yew 'Brandon'
Taxus sp. 'Morden'

Also known as 'Morden,' this yew is
a bit difficult to find but worth the
search. Extremely hardy. Very attractive
in shaded rock gardens. A slow-growing plant with soft, dark green foliage.
Height: 30–60cm; width: 60–90cm.
Shade to A.M. sun.

Dogwood 'Ivory Halo'

Hydrangea 'Kyushu'

American Alumroot (Dale's strain)

Large rocks make excellent landscaping features, but care must be taken to complement them with plants.

I have a large, gorgeous boulder in the middle of my front yard. I would like to highlight it with plants. What grows here?

BECAUSE BOULDERS have such striking presence, consider topiary, weeping plants or ones with strong forms to highlight this feature. Look carefully at the shade and texture of the rock, and choose complementary plant foliage and colours to create impact.

ANNUALS

Amaranthus 'Love Lies Bleeding'
Amaranthus caudatus
A superb feature plant that is striking in backgrounds. Long, dark red, trailing rope-like flowers make interesting cutflowers. Height: 90–150cm; spacing: 35–45cm. Sun.

Canna Lily 'Wine 'n' Roses'
Attractive dark burgundy foliage will form a large clump and offers contrast in containers and gardens. This bulb can be lifted and overwintered. Produces huge, deep-rose flowers. Height: 1m. Sun.

Rudbeckia 'Indian Summer'
Superb in mass displays, borders and containers. Produces loads of deep golden, semi-double, 15–25cm, daisy-like flowers with brown centres. Excellent cutflower. Height: 50cm; spacing: 30cm. Sun.

Rudbeckia 'Indian Summer'

Amaranthus 'Love Lies Bleeding'

Canna Lily 'Wine 'n' Roses'

Jacob's Ladder

PERENNIALS

Daylily
Hemerocallis 'Pocket Change'

A shorter daylily for the front of the border. Bright red flowers with a lighter edge bloom in late June to early July. Clump-forming—divide every 3–5 years to maintain vigour. Prefers moist, fertile, well-drained soil. Height: 45cm; width: 30–60cm. Sun to P.M. sun.

Jacob's Ladder
Polemonium caeruleum

Fern-like foliage on a clump-forming plant with blue flowers in late spring to early summer—deadhead after blooming. Plant in a border or woodland garden. Self-sows freely. Deadhead after blooming. Prefers moist, fertile, well-drained soil. Height: 45–90cm; width: 30–45cm. Sun to P.M. sun.

Western Sage
Artemisia ludoviciana 'Silver Queen'

Thriving in a hot and dry location, this clump-forming perennial displays silver-grey foliage that contrasts beautifully with rock. Foliage can be dried.

Daylily 'Pocket Change'

Prune back hard in spring. Does best in well-drained, alkaline, poor, dry soil. Height: 60–75cm; width: 60–90+cm. Sun.

TREES & SHRUBS

Pine 'Eastern Weeping White'
Pinus strobus 'Pendula'

Can be allowed to weep and trail over rocks or walls—excellent feature. Size varies tremendously because of its very attractive and erratic weeping growth habit. Soft bluish-green foliage and pendulous branches. Height: 4–9m; width: 3–4m. Sun.

Pine 'Hillside Creeper'
Pinus sylvestris

Grows around rocks and spills over walls—a spectacular feature. Can be used as an attractive groundcover. Considered a fast-growing evergreen. Height: 30–60cm; width: 2–3m. Sun.

Spruce 'Weeping Norway'
Picea abies 'Pendula'

A versatile feature plant, that can be grown as a living fence, groundcover, screen, or climbing rocks and walls. Displays dark green, dense growth on an extremely pendulous, striking form. Can be staked to grow taller. Height: training dependent; width: 4–6m. Sun to P.M. sun.

Sumac 'Laceleaf Staghorn'
Rhus typhina 'Laciniata'

Finely dissected leaves produce a lacy tropical look—interesting for screens and accents. Beautiful orange-red fall colour. Height: 2–3m; width: 4–5m. Sun to P.M. sun.

Pine 'Hillside Creeper'

Pine 'Eastern Weeping White'

Spruce 'Weeping Norway'

The colour and fragrance of 'Cuthbertson Floribunda Mix' sweet peas will greet anyone passing through this gate.

We have a painted front gate with a wide arbour arching over it. We would like to cover it with interesting plants. What grows here?

ARBOURS ARE A VERY welcoming feature and traditionally they support climbing vines, roses or even a combination of the two. If you love this look, keep in mind that the arbour must be wide enough to allow for passage, without brushing up against thorns. Annual vines offer good coverage and the option of changing the look every year.

ANNUALS

Cup and Saucer Vine 'Purple'
Cobaea scandens
A fast-growing annual vine that is wind tolerant. Large flowers open light-green maturing to purple and are cup-shaped. Height: up to 3m; spacing: 25–30cm. Sun.

Sweet Pea, Cuthbertson Floribunda Series
This series blooms prolifically with sweetly-scented flowers borne on long stems, making excellent cutflowers. Available in maroon, rose-pink, scarlet, white and a mix. Requires support. Height: 2m. Sun.

FRUIT

Kiwi 'Arctic Beauty'

The male kiwi is a very showy climber with attractive pink, white and green foliage. The female plants are less showy, with solid green foliage, but still very attractive and, with the male to pollinate, produce small, novelty fruit in September. Fruit production is not reliable. Height: 2+m; width: 1–1.5m. Shade to A.M. sun.

PERENNIALS

Alpine Clematis

Clematis alpina 'Francis Rivis'

Produces a lush, pest-free screen early in spring. Grow as a very hardy climber with support, groundcover or trailing over stone walls. Produces nodding, blue flowers with a white centre in spring. Requires fertile, well-drained soil and cool roots. Do not cut back. Height: 2–3m; width: 2m. Sun to P.M. sun.

Honeysuckle 'Gold Flame'

Lonicera x *heckrottii*

This climbing vine requires support and produces pink, sweetly-scented, tubular blooms with a yellow throat in July. Do not cut back in fall. Height: 3–4m; width: 1–2m. Sun to P.M. sun.

Perennial Sweet Pea

Lathyrus latifolius

Grow through trees or shrubs or as a groundcover over a bank. Needs support to climb. Cut down in fall. Blue-green foliage. White, pink or rose-red flowers bloom summer to fall. Prefers fertile, well-drained, organic soil. Height: 2–3m; width: 60–90cm. Sun to P.M. sun.

ROSES

'Captain Samuel Holland'
Explorer *Shrub*

A climbing rose with lots of flowers in clusters of up to 10. Hardy to Zone 3. Double, medium red, 7cm flowers; blooms early summer to frost. Light fragrance. Height: 2m; spread: 1–1.5m. Sun.

Rose 'Captain Samuel Holland'

Alpine Clematis 'Francis Rivis'

Perennial Sweet Pea

Spend some time designing your free-standing trellis so that it will be attractive on its own.

I have installed a long stretch of free-standing trellis to screen out an unattractive view in my sunny backyard. I would like to cover the trellis with vines that have pretty blooms, interesting seed heads or foliage. What grows here?

THERE ARE NUMEROUS interesting vines that will create an effective privacy screen. Vines come in three basic categories: those that come back from old wood every year; those that die back to ground level each fall and grow back in spring; and annuals. Some of these are more labour intensive than others, so select one according to the amount of time you intend to spend planting, pruning and caring for that vine.

FRUIT

Grape 'Valiant'
Vitis

A popular and hardy grape producing deep blue, 1cm fruit in early August.

Excellent for wines, juice and jellies. Height: training dependent. Sun.

PERENNIALS

Golden Clematis
Clematis tangutica 'Golden Harvest'

This is the largest, hardiest and most vigorous clematis. It climbs on support and also makes a great groundcover for slopes or banks. Gold-yellow flowers bloom from mid summer to fall, followed by attractive seedheads. Prune back ⅓rd of growth in spring. Prefers well-drained soil. Height: 3–4m; width: 2–3m. Sun to P.M. sun.

Vine Bower
Clematis viticella 'Blue Angel'

Makes a hardy, lush, pest-free and easy to grow screen. It needs a support and cool roots. Clear blue flowers bloom from summer to fall. Cut back in late fall. Thrives in fertile, well-drained soil. Height: 3–3.5m; width: 1–2m. Sun to P.M. sun.

VEGETABLES

Cucumber 'Diva'

An award-winning variety with a vining habit and high yields. A superb, self-pollinating salad cucumber with smooth, thin skin—no peeling required. Produces sweetly-flavoured, semi-glossy, 15–20cm, slender, burpless and seedless cucumbers. Sun.

Scarlet Runner Bean

A very ornamental and vigorous pole bean. The vines sport scarlet flowers followed by green, 15cm beans. Can grow up poles, trellises and fences. Late July to early August harvest. Height: 2+m. Sun.

Scarlet Runner Bean

Grape 'Valiant'

Golden Clematis 'Golden Harvest'

Vine Bower 'Blue Angel'

Trellises & Arbours

Espallier is the art of training plants on a lattice or framework. It takes time and patience, but this 'Battleford' apple shows the striking results.

I have a sunny, trellised area at the side of my house and would really like to try my hand at training and pruning a shrub or tree up against it. What grows here?

THE PROCESS OF TRAINING a tree or shrub to a horizontally branching form requires a great deal of patience and careful pruning. Depending on the plant you choose, it will take several years before your plant reaches the desired form. If you are committed, however, you can effectively train a range of trees, small shrubs, roses and even vines into interesting forms and patterns.

FRUIT

Apple 'Battleford'
Malus
Apples are fast-growing trees that can be trained quite easily. Battleford produces red with green stripes, 7–8cm, crisp and tasty fruit in early September. Good in desserts and fair for cooking, as well as a fair keeper. Sun.

ROSES

'Red Leaf Rose'
Species
This hardy shrub rose grows quickly, flowers in clusters and has striking reddish-purple foliage with a blue cast. Produces single, mauve pink, 3–4cm flowers in mid to late June with a light, fruity fragrance. Height: 1.5–2m; spread: 1.5m. Sun.

TREES & SHRUBS

Juniper 'Savin'
Juniperus sabina

A distinct vase-shaped, dense form that is great in large shrub beds. Can be trained into an interesting fan shape. Very dark green foliage turns much paler in winter. Height: 1.5m; width: 1.5–3m. Sun.

Maple 'Amur'
Acer tataricum ssp. *ginnala*

Easily trained to many forms—a beautiful feature for small yards. Fragrant blooms in spring. A small, wide-spreading tree with orange-red fall colour and red, winged seeds. Height: 4–6m; width: 5m. Sun to P.M. sun.

Ornamental Crabapple 'Makamik'
Malus

This fast-growing tree is spectacular in bloom and provides interesting contrast in the garden. It has bronze leaves, produces dark red flower buds that open to purple-red blooms and 1–2cm, purple-red fruit. Blooms in late May to early June. Height: 10m; width: 10m. Sun.

Sea Buckthorn
Hippophae rhamnoides 'Frugana'

This female plant has masses of bright orange berries in fall, lasting all winter; requires a male pollinator. Can be a grown as a small tree or shrub, or trained against a wall. Displays dense, willow-like, silvery grey foliage. Height: 3–6m; width: 3–6m. Sun.

Trellises & Arbours

Juniper 'Savin'

Ornamental Crabapple 'Makamik'

Maple 'Amur'

Pergolas should be integrated into the landscape by growing plants up, on and around them.

We have just built a patio with a pergola stretching over it in a very sunny part of our yard. We placed flowerbeds on three sides of the pergola in the hope that we can create some shade with plants. What grows here?

To create shade and cover the pillars and overhead beams of your pergola, place a small tree in the southern-most bed and plant thick vines at the base of the posts. It will take time before you have the degree of shade you desire, so hang large baskets of blooming and trailing annuals in strategic locations to create an interim solution.

ANNUALS

Bacopa 'Abunda Giant White'

Bacopa is heat tolerant and good in hanging baskets and mixed planters. Hundreds of white, single flowers bloom on a low-growing and fast-spreading plant. Height: 5–10cm; trails to 20cm. Sun.

Calibrachoa, Million Bells Series

A fast-growing, heavy-blooming and self-cleaning plant that thrives in hanging baskets, containers, or grown as an annual groundcover. Small, petunia-like blooms cover the entire trailing plant. Height: 8–15cm; trails to 60cm. Sun.

Geranium 'Galleria Sunrise'

This geranium has an outstanding mounding and trailing habit and large, bright scarlet-orange flowers. Excellent in hanging baskets and containers. Height: 30–35cm. Sun to P.M. sun.

PERENNIALS

Alpine Clematis
Clematis alpina 'Frankie'

Produces a lush, pest-free screen early in spring. Grow as a very hardy climber with support, groundcover or trailing over stone walls. Produces nodding, blue-purple flowers in spring. Requires fertile, well-drained soil and cool roots. Do not cut back. Height: 3m; width: 2m. Sun to P.M. sun.

TREES & SHRUBS

Dogwood 'Pagoda'
Cornus alternifolia

Tiered branches naturally create an open form—grow in an area with adequate space. Spectacular in bloom with creamy flowers in late spring. Red and purple fall colour and attractive in form in winter Height: 4–7m; width: 6–10m. Sun to P.M. sun.

Ornamental Crabapple 'Thunderchild'
Malus x *pumila*

A striking, fast-growing tree with beautiful, deep purple-red foliage. Very resistant to fireblight. An excellent size for small yards. Produces deep pink blooms in spring followed by small, dark reddish-purple fruit. Height: 6–7m; width: 5–7m. Sun.

Serviceberry 'Autumn Brilliance'
Amelanchier x *grandiflora*

A great tree for small yards. Pretty pinkish-white blooms appear in spring. Puts on a great display of incredible red fall colour. Avoid windy sites. Height: 6–7m; width: 4–6m. Sun to P.M. sun.

Ornamental Crabapple 'Thunderchild'

Bacopa 'Abunda Giant White'

Serviceberry 'Autumn Brilliance'

10
Sharing
the Garden

…sharing with Emma
sometimes means compromising…

There are so many reasons that gardening gives us satisfaction, and for most of us it's the joy of sharing the results of our hard work with others, be they insect, animal or human. I share my garden with my daughter Emma—but sharing with her often means compromising.

One summer, the lawn in my backyard played host to a large slime mould. Some would say that it was a pretty gruesome guest, but Emma found it fascinating. So I mowed around the mould, leaving it in peace until Emma found something else to catch her attention.

I admit that I get a kick out of her interest in the natural world—she's not at all squeamish about the bugs we encounter—but I'd guess our view on sharing might be different from yours. My boundaries are flexible enough to tolerate a slime mould for a while. Other gardeners may not be so forgiving. To them, sharing the garden means planting flowers that will attract birds and honeybees—but no wasps or deer, please. The reality is, gardens are chock full of tasty morsels that all sorts of interesting creatures are going to find irresistible, even if all you have is an expanse of lawn.

Mom and Dad raised me to believe in sharing. Neither had much enthusiasm for going after the various pests that raided our gardens. And when kids snuck into our market gardens to snatch a few peas, well, we just thought of that as part of the cost of doing business.

There are a few independent souls who garden strictly for themselves, content to raise roses or perennials untouched by any eyes save their own. But I think most of us garden with an audience in mind, whether it be our neighbours, visiting friends and relatives, or people strolling along the sidewalk. So if a few pests sneak in, well, there's usually room enough for them too, as long as their numbers are reasonably small and they don't overstay their welcome.

In the end, I think sharing the garden is about compromising. That may involve leaving a strip of lawn for the dog to lie on or, in my case, putting up with a patch of slime mould to satisfy an inquiring young mind. Sharing our space—with people, pets or even pests—is one of the biggest rewards of gardening. ❧

A well-balanced bed will combine evergreens such as 'Blue Star' juniper with a variety of blooming plants.

A group of us share a sunny community bed located in front of our condominium units. We want to plant a combination of plants that will provide interest all year and be easy for the group to maintain. What grows here?

A WELL-DESIGNED BED used in commercial or large residential landscaping should consist of plants that require minimal pruning and watering and are disease and pest resistant. Choose plants accordingly and in a range of heights, colours (both bloom and foliage), blooming times and different forms to provide impact and interest. Use a repetitive theme when planting, as this is a simple way to coordinate the group effort and will create balance, proportion and continuity of design.

ANNUALS

Rudbeckia 'Sonora'
Superb in mass displays, borders and containers, as well as an excellent cutflower. Golden-yellow, rusty-red centred,10–15cm daisy-like flowers. Height: 30–35cm; spacing: 30cm. Sun.

PERENNIALS

Peony
Paeonia 'Gay Paree'
Peonies are slow growing but long-lived perennials. This Japanese form produces striking magenta flowers with creamy centres in spring. Plant eyes 5cm deep. Requires moist, acid-free, fertile, well-drained soil. Height: 110cm; width: 90–100cm. Sun to P.M. sun.

Spike Speedwell
Veronica 'Sunny Border Blue'

An award-winning variety that makes an excellent long-blooming plant for the mixed border. Spiked, violet-blue flowers appear in summer on a clump-forming, compact plant. Deadhead for more blooms and do not over fertilize. Prefers organic, moist, well-drained soil. Height: 45–50cm; width: 30–45cm. Sun to P.M. sun.

ROSES

'Cuthbert Grant' Parkland
Hardy Shrub

This rose displays clusters of big, showy flowers in tight buds like a hybrid tea. Experiences little, if any, winterkill and requires minimal pruning. Hardy to Zone 2. Semi-double, dark crimson, 10cm roses bloom late June through summer with a light fragrance. Height: 1m; spread: 1m. Sun.

Rose 'Cuthbert Grant'

Rudbeckia 'Sonora'

TREES & SHRUBS

Juniper 'Blue Star'
Juniperus squamata

Very bright blue foliage on a slow-growing, rounded bush that does not require pruning. Best with good snow cover through winter. Dislikes high humidity. Height: 90cm; width: 1–1.5m. Sun.

Ninebark 'Diabolo'
Physocarpus opulifolius

Great for large shrub beds or for use as a hedge. A super contrast plant with rich purple foliage on strong, upright growth and pink clustered blooms in summer. Height: 2–3m; width: 2–3m. Sun to A.M. sun.

Pine 'Big Tuna'
Pinus mugo

This attractive pine provides form contrast in large beds. A striking, oval shape with a very dense, compact habit that does not require shearing. Height: 3–4m; width: 2–3m. Sun.

Pine 'Big Tuna'

Brighten boulevards and sidewalks with happy colours like those of 'Bon Bon Orange' calendula.

We have an unhealthy strip of old, struggling grass on the boulevard in front of our home and would like to replace it with a mixed planting. This area receives afternoon light only. What grows here?

BOULEVARDS FALL UNDER the jurisdiction of municipalities and often permission must be granted to plant in this space. That being said, many forward-thinking municipalities are willing to allow home-owners to serve as partners in watering and maintenance tasks and the beautification of streetscapes. Be aware that the plants used in this site will need to be tolerant of snow load, salt and indiscriminate foot traffic.

ANNUALS

Calendula, Bon Bon Series
Very easy to grow and excellent in mass displays and as a cutflower. Mix includes double flowers in bright orange, apricot and bright and pale yellow. Height: 25–30cm; spacing: 20cm. Sun.

Poppy, Shirley Types
Excellent in mass displays. Double or single delicate flowers in shades of pink, red, salmon and scarlet. Allow to self-seed. Height: 40–50cm; spacing: 20–30cm. Sun.

PERENNIALS

Himalayan Cinquefoil
Potentilla 'Gibson's Scarlet'

A herbaceous version of the popular shrub—tough and long blooming. Use as a clump-forming groundcover. Single, scarlet-red flowers bloom in summer. Tolerates hot and dry locations but prefers well-drained, poor to moderately fertile soil. Height: 30–45cm; width: 45–60cm. Sun.

Lupine
Lupinus polyphyllus

Clump-forming plants with spiked, summer-blooming flowers, available in vibrant colours. Best in cool summers. Prefers well-drained, moderately fertile, sandy and slightly acidic soil. Height: 75–150cm; width: 30–40cm. Sun to P.M. sun.

TREES & SHRUBS

Potentilla 'Abbotswood'
Potentilla fruticosa

Masses of bright white blooms cover this shrub in summer. Makes a great border plant and can be used for hedging. Height: 90cm; width: 90–100cm. Sun.

Spiraea 'Magic Carpet'
Spiraea japonica

A great, low-growing contrast plant that produces red, yellow and pink foliage and pink blooms in June and July. Shearing plants after blooming encourages branching and fresh new colour. Height: 25–30cm; width: 60–90cm. Sun.

Himalayan Cinquefoil 'Gibson's Scarlet'

Potentilla 'Abbotswood'

Lupine

Poppy, Shirley Type

The fruits of European mountain ash attract birds and provide much-needed food for those that do not migrate in fall.

We have well-established trees on our boulevard that attract many types of wild birds. We do not have much landscaping in our slightly shady lot and we would like to incorporate some plants to entice the local birds into our yard. What grows here?

BIRDS REQUIRE COVER and perches, water and food. Select plants whose fruit and seeds are a natural draw and use evergreens and woody deciduous plants to create a supportive environment that will keep birds visiting year-round.

ANNUALS

Ornamental Millet 'Purple Majesty'
Pennisetum glaucum
Dark purple foliage and cattail-like, deep purple, 20–30cm seed heads give height to containers and garden beds. Superb as a backdrop. Great dried or fresh cutflower. Height: 120–150cm; spacing: 30cm. Sun to P.M. sun.

FRUIT

Cherry 'Nanking'
Prunus tomentosa
Often used as an ornamental for hedges or trained to a small tree form, this cherry displays pretty, pale-pink blooms in early spring followed by red, 2cm, sweet fruit in July. Can yield from 4–11kg per plant—cross pollinates with other cherries and plums. Height: 2–3m; width: 2–3m. Sun.

PERENNIALS

Feather Reed Grass
Calamagrostis x *acutiflora* 'Overdam'

An elegant grass in a very erect, non-spreading clump form. Leave standing through winter as it will stay upright and provide an attractive accent. Variegated foliage with pink seed heads in late summer. Prefers moist, organic soil. Height: 75–120cm; width: 30–45cm. Sun to P.M. sun.

TREES & SHRUBS

Cedar 'Brandon'
Thuja occidentalis

Medium to dark green, dense foliage provides coverage for birds. Use as a feature, singly or grouped. Makes a good screen. Best in a moist, humid site. Height: 9–10m; width: 2–3m. Sun to P.M. sun.

Hazelnut 'American'
Corylus americana

Edible fruits mature in the fall, attracting birds and squirrels. Use this shrub for screens, informal hedges and naturalizing. Displays showy catkins in the spring. Height: 3–5m; width: 2–3m. Sun to P.M. sun.

European Mountain Ash
Sorbus acuparia

A number of bird species enjoy the fruits of this tree throughout the winter. Dense, oval-headed and available in single or multi-stemmed forms, it produces clustered, white spring blooms followed by orange-red fruit. Lovely fall colour. Great for small yards. Requires well-drained soil. Height: 7–10m; width: 5–7m. Sun.

Wildlife

Feather Reed Grass 'Overdam'

Hazelnut 'American'

Cedar 'Brandon'

*Mixed plantings of successively blooming plants will attract butterflies through the warm months.
'De La Mina' verbena flowers all summer and will tolerate a light frost.*

For years I have tended a small vegetable garden in my
backyard. Since I am no longer able to plant it each year,
I would like to instead fill in the area with flowers and
shrubs that attract butterflies. What grows here?

URNING A VEGETABLE PATCH into a flower garden is an easy task.
The ground should already be well-tilled and the soil rich—conditions that will successfully nurture a variety of blooming plants that attract
butterflies. Choose flowering shrubs, reliable perennials and self-seeding
annuals to eliminate yearly replanting. Add charm and a spot to enjoy your
blooms and their winged visitors by including a comfortable place to sit in
your design.

ANNUALS

Verbena 'De La Mina'

A sun-loving and free-flowering, trailing verbena that produces dark-purple
buds that open to vibrant lilac, fragrant
flowers. Upright, mounding and well-
branched, as well as drought tolerant.
Height: 30cm; spreads to 90cm. Sun.

Cosmos, Sonata Series

Giant, daisy-like single flowers on compact, free-flowering plants. Available in shades of pink, red, rose and white, 10cm flowers that make great cutflowers. Good in hot, dry sites. Height: 60cm; spacing: 30–40cm. Sun.

Dianthus, Super Parfait Series

Very attractive grown en masse in borders and garden beds. Huge 4cm, lacy fringed flowers with distinct eyes, available in raspberry or strawberry shades. Quite frost tolerant. Height: 15–20cm; spacing: 15–20cm. Sun.

Petunia, Double Wave Series

Superb in hanging baskets, containers and mass displays. 'Double Wave White' produces loads of pure white, 5–6cm, double flowers. Vigorous growth habit. Height: 25–40cm; spreads to 60–90cm. Sun to P.M. sun.

Petunia 'Double Wave White'

Cosmos 'Sonata Pink'

PERENNIALS

Blanket Flower
Gaillardia 'Baby Cole'
A longer-lived, clump-forming dwarf gaillardia that tolerates poor soils and attracts butterflies. Cut back in fall to aid in overwintering. Red and yellow flowers with maroon centers bloom in summer. Prefers fertile, well-drained, dry soil. Height: 15–20cm; width: 15–20cm. Sun to P.M. sun.

Coneflower
Echinacea purpurea 'Magnus'
An award-winning variety with petals that are more horizontal than other coneflowers. Flat, purple flowers with dark orange disks bloom summer to fall on a clump-forming plant. Drought tolerant once established. Prefers well-drained soil. Height: 60–90cm; width: 45cm. Sun to P.M. sun.

Garden Phlox
Phlox paniculata 'Starfire'
Offset by dark green foliage, fragrant crimson-red flowers bloom in mid summer on a plant with an upright habit. One of the best bright red phlox available. It may require staking. Do not crowd and always water at its base. Best in moist, fertile, well-drained soil. Height: 75–90cm; width 75–90cm. Sun to P.M. sun.

Small Globe Thistle
Echinops ritro
A heat and drought-tolerant addition to a border or wild garden. Silver-grey foliage is clump forming and compact in habit. Blue flowers appearing in late summer attract butterflies and are excellent for cutting and drying. Thrives in poor, well-drained soil. Height: 60cm; width: 45cm. Sun to P.M. sun.

Blanket Flower 'Baby Cole'

Garden Phlox 'Starfire'

Small Globe Thistle

Painted Daisy

Tanacetum coccineum 'James Kelway'

Pretty, single, daisy-like, crimson-pink flowers with yellow centres bloom on this upright perennial in early summer. Makes an excellent cut flower. Cut back after flowering for second flush of blooms. Prefers well-drained soil. Height: 45–60cm; width: 30–45cm. Sun to P.M. sun.

TREES & SHRUBS

Honeysuckle 'Sweetberry'

Lonicera caerulea

An ideal small shrub for beds or foundation plantings with dense bright green foliage and yellowish-white spring blooms, followed by sweet, edible fruit. Prefers moist soil. Height: 1–1.5m; width: 1–1.5m. Sun to P.M. sun.

Lilac 'Tinkerbelle'

Syringa vulgaris 'President Grevy'

Rich wine red buds open to deep pink, spicy-scented blooms in June. Compact foliage, upright growth and a non-suckering habit make this shrub great as a feature or grown as a hedge. Height: 1.5–2m; width: 1.5m. Sun to P.M. sun.

Mockorange 'Miniature Snowflake'

Philadelphus

Great as an informal hedge or feature shrub. Prolific, double, white, fragrant blooms appear in June. Height: 60–90cm; width: 30–60cm. Sun to P.M. sun.

Wildlife

Painted Daisy 'James Kelway'

Mockorange 'Miniature Snowflake'

Honeysuckle 'Sweetberry'

With a few simple selections, you can beautify the kids' play structure and introduce them to the joy of gardening.

Our children's two-level play structure in our backyard sticks out like a sore thumb. We'd like to camouflage it with plants that stand up to kids, but still let us see them. What grows here?

PLANT CLIMBING VINES to grow on the structure and soften its edges with a large shrub, making sure to avoid those that are delicate, thorny or have poisonous parts. If the play structure is quite large, disguising it with these plants may take several years—in the interim, fill beds, containers and window boxes with interesting, colourful and trailing annuals that get the kids involved in gardening too.

ANNUALS

Amaranthus 'Pygmy Torch'

An exotic-looking plant that adds dramatic contrast to pots and flowerbeds. Kids love the 30cm, upright, crimson flowers. Warm location is a must for success. Height: 60cm. Sun.

Bells of Ireland

A novel accent with apple-green, bell-shaped flowers that make ideal dried flowers. Height: 60cm; spacing: 25–30cm. Sun to P.M. sun.

Marigold, Bonanza Series

A heat tolerant plant that's easy to grow an is excellent in mass displays, containers and borders. Available in a wide range of colours. Large 5cm, double flowers. Height: 20cm; spacing: 15–20cm. Sun to P.M. sun.

Amaranthus 'Pygmy Torch'

Marigold 'Bonanza Mix'

Bells of Ireland

Kids

Nepeta Vine 'Variegated'
& Begonia 'Non-Stop Rose Pink'

Nepeta Vine

Excellent in containers or as an annual groundcover. Available in variegated green and white or solid green foliage. A vigorous plant with round, aromatic foliage. Trails to 1–2m. Sun to P.M. sun.

Sunflower 'Mammoth Russian'

Kids love to see how big this variety will get with its enormous yellow flowers on sturdy stalks that can reach 2m in height. Easy, fast and rewarding to grow. Sun.

FRUIT

Cherry 'Carmine Jewel'

Prunus x *kerrasis*

An extremely hardy, self-pollinating introduction from Saskatchewan that is both beautiful and practical. Highly ornamental, white blooms in spring are followed by fruit with dark red skin and flesh in mid July to mid August—great for processing. Height: 2–3m; width: 2–3m. Sun.

Sumac 'Cutleaf Smooth'

PERENNIALS

Alpine Clematis
Clematis alpina 'Constance'

Produces a lush, pest-free screen early in spring. Grow as a very hardy climber with support, groundcover or trailing over stone walls. Pretty, semi-double, purple-pink flowers bloom in spring. Requires fertile, well-drained soil and cool roots. Do not cut back. Height: 2–3m; width: 2m. Sun to P.M. sun.

Goat's Beard
Aruncus dioicus

Great in a woodland garden or in the back of a shady border, this big plant has a bushy habit with lush green foliage and feathery white plumes in late spring to early summer. Requires moist, fertile soil. Height: 1–1.5m; width: 90cm–100cm. Shade to A.M. sun.

TREES & SHRUBS

Sumac 'Cutleaf Smooth'
Rhus glabra 'Lacinata'

Glossy, smooth bark and lacy, tropical-like foliage make this a great plant for screening. Strategically prune to allow views. Green blooms appear in late spring. Provides incredible orange-red fall colour with deep-scarlet seed clusters. Height: 3–5m; width: 3–5m. Sun to P.M. sun.

VEGETABLES

Pea 'Knight'

Kids love to grow things that they can eat. Grow this vining pea variety up a support. Produces green, 10 cm long, double podded (produces 2 pods per flower) peas that are harvested early. Height: 60cm. Sun.

Kids

Goat's Beard

11

A Little
Architecture

…take your eyes off the ground…

Here's a little fact of life I'd like to share: all of us tend to take the easy route to success. If we lived in a world of instant gratification, we'd all enjoy fantastic gardens with no more effort than scattering seed around the yard. And I'll admit that sometimes I wouldn't mind if the garden were a little less work; but it is often a case of doing a little work now or doing a lot of work later.

The savvy gardener won't want to miss the opportunity to create his or her own architectural features. For example, you may decide to deal with trouble spots like slopes with terracing and retaining walls, or to deal with poor locations by adding raised planters. In the short run, these solutions may not be the easiest, nor the cheapest, routes to success, but they certainly can be spectacular when the work is all finished.

Of course, this approach takes definite planning, and more than a few hours of manual labour. But the extra effort will be worth it. There's no aesthetic sacrifice made when you raise plants up off the ground; in fact, their beauty is often enhanced. In the case of the raised beds, bringing plants up to waist level means that you don't have to endure bending as much to plant, water, weed and harvest the garden. Raising the soil level lowers the pain in your back and knees—a boon to gardeners with mobility problems. I find amending the soil in raised beds easier, and some beds and retaining walls actually raise the temperature of the garden, providing a new micro-climate with which to experiment.

When trying to decide what grows where in your yard, take your eyes off the ground and set your sights just a little higher. It may take a little more work, but in the end the answer to "What grows here?" isn't nearly as important as how you approached the question in the first place. ⚘

Use 'Amazon Sunset' lotus vine and 'Non-Stop Mix' begonias to provide colour and contrast seasonally or just until other plants have reached a substantial size.

The high retaining wall running the length of my driveway is really boring and, quite frankly, ugly. I'd like to grow something up it or trail something down over its face. What grows here?

PLANT A VARIETY OF climbing plants at the base of the wall and allow them to cover the unattractive face. You may need to add support, such as a trellis or wire. Since you can plant on top of the wall, use plants that naturally trail. Plants with arching habits can be trained to cover the wall by placing weights on the ends of the branches. You could also mount attractive containers directly onto the wall, filled with bright flowers and tumbling vines.

ANNUALS

Lotus Vine 'Amazon Sunset'
Lotus maculatus
Adds fullness and texture to any container. Excellent in hanging baskets, containers and mixed planters. Occasionally produces scarlet-red, beak-like flowers. Soft, needle-like, silvery-green, airy foliage. Trails to 90cm. Sun.

PERENNIALS

Vine Bower
Clematis viticella 'African Girl'
Makes a hardy, lush, pest-free and easy to grow screen. It needs a support and cool roots. Dark purple flowers bloom in summer followed by very attractive seedheads. Cut back in late fall. Thrives in fertile, well-drained soil. Height: 2.5–3.5m; width: 1–2m. Sun to P.M. sun.

ROSES

'Marie Victorin' Explorer *Shrub*

This rose displays a lovely arching
habit. Single, peachy-pink, 5–7cm
flowers bloom from late June through
summer with a light fragrance. Height:
1m; spread: 1.5m. Sun.

'The Polar Star' *Hardy Shrub*

Not for the faint of heart, this vigorous climber has formidable thorns but
really covers a large expanse. Thin out
canes regularly. Blooms in early summer with semi-double, pure white,
2–3cm, unscented flowers. Height:
4–6m; spread: 2–3m. Sun.

TREES & SHRUBS

Juniper 'Prince of Wales'
Juniperus horizantalis

A great groundcover that drapes over
walls and around rocks. Lovely in rock
gardens. Fast growing with trailing
branches and bright green foliage that
often turns purplish in winter. Height:
10–15cm; width: 3–4m. Sun.

Pine 'Hillside Creeper'

Juniper 'Prince of Wales'

Spruce 'Weeping Blue'
Picea pungens 'Pendula'

A unique feature tree cascading over
rocks and walls—can be used as a
groundcover. Blue foliage highlights
downward angled branches. Training is
required to produce desired height and
effect. Height: train up to 4–5m; width:
1–1.5m in 15 years. Sun to P.M. sun.

Spiraea 'Bridalwreath'
Spiraea prunifolia

Extremely showy when in flower,
branches arch and are smothered in
tiny, white blooms in spring. Great
addition to shrub beds. Height: 1–3m;
width: 2–3m. Sun to P.M. sun.

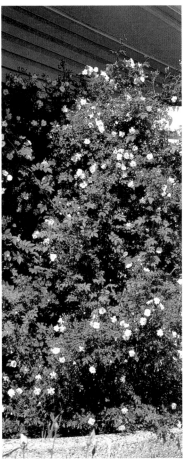

Rose 'The Polar Star'

'Wilton's Blue Rug' juniper spills over rocks and walls and still stands up to the rigours of a hot location.

We have multiple terraces that are fronted by low retaining walls extending up the slope of our landscape. The beds are each only about 90cm wide. It's very sunny and very hot. What grows here?

CAREFULLY CONSIDER HOW you view this location and the difficulty of access. Because you face this slope from the bottom, place taller plant selections midway up the slope. This will provide shade on the hill and will look proportionally correct amidst a variety of other plants, themselves alternating between upright, mounding and creeping or weeping forms. If access to your terraces is difficult, choose plants that require little maintenance and supplemental watering (unless you are prepared to install an irrigation system).

ANNUALS

Portulaca, Sundial Series

Portulaca thrive in hot, dry rock gardens and borders. 4–5cm, rose-like flowers bloom in shades of yellow, cream, orange and mango. Height: 15cm; spacing: 10–15cm. Sun.

PERENNIALS

Dwarf Balloon Flower

Platycodon grandiflorus 'Sentimental Blue'

This clump-forming plant produces flower buds that swell up like balloons before opening to star-like, purple-blue flowers in summer. It is very late to come up in the spring and dislikes being moved. Prefers deep, fertile, well-drained soil in a hot location and tolerates periods of drought. Height: 10–20cm; width: 20–30cm. Sun.

Hen and Chicks
Sempervivum

Drought-tolerant, evergreen, succulent rosettes form mats that are wonderful for edging or in rock gardens. Available in different shades of grey, green and brown. Flowers may be white, yellow, red or purple and bloom in summer. Thrives in poor to moderately fertile, sharply-drained, gritty soil—avoid winter wet. Height: 5–20cm; width: 15–30cm. Sun.

Maiden Pink
Dianthus deltoides 'Brilliant'

Double, bright crimson flowers bloom in summer on an evergreen, mat-forming plant—do not cut back. Self-sows freely. Prefers moist, well-drained, alkaline soil—avoid winter wet. Height: 15–20cm; width: 25–45cm. Sun to P.M. sun.

Serbian Bellflower
Campanula poscharskyana
'Blue Waterfall'

A vigorous plant that spreads by underground runners and produces blue flowers summer to fall. Grows well on banks and in wild or rock gardens. Thrives in fertile, well-drained, moist

soil. Height: 8–15cm; width: 30–60cm. Sun to A.M. sun.

TREES & SHRUBS

Juniper 'Wilton's Blue Rug'
Juniperus horizantalis 'Wiltonii'

A hardy and fast growing juniper with trailing branches and silver-blue foliage tinged purple in winter. Wide spreading and tolerant of hard soil. Height: 10–15cm; width: 2–3m. Sun.

Spruce 'Creeping Blue'
Picea pungens 'Glauca Procumbens'

This spruce can be trained to climb over rocks and small walls—an excellent choice for large rock gardens. Bright silvery-blue needles form a dense, slow-growing mat. Height: 30–60cm; width: 4–6m. Sun.

Spruce 'Creeping Blue'

Serbian Bellflower 'Blue Waterfall'

Hen and Chicks

Russian cypress provides spreading coverage and year-round interest in shadier areas.

Our shaded front yard slopes down to the street and has deep, bare sections carved into terracing. We do not have a lot of time for maintenance, but would like to create some visual interest. What grows here?

SWATHS OF ONE SINGLE TYPE of plant are the simplest treatment in this type of setting and, if you choose a plant that doesn't require pruning and is drought tolerant, also the lowest maintenance option. Mixed plantings, however, provide all-season interest and offer more ways in which to use bright colours and variegated foliage, which is striking in a shady location.

ANNUALS

Mimulus, Mystic Series
Attractive in mass displays, borders and hanging baskets. This unique plant can grow almost anywhere. 5cm, open snapdragon-like flowers available in a range of colours. Height: 20–25cm; spacing: 15–20cm. Sun or shade.

PERENNIALS

Japanese Spurge
Pachysandra terminalis 'Variegata'
A densely carpeting groundcover—great for damp, shady areas. This variety is slower growing than the species. White and green foliage highlights white flowers in early summer. Prefers moist soil—avoid dry sites. Height: 15–20cm; width: 60–90+cm. Shade to A.M. sun.

Longleaf Lungwort
Pulmonaria 'Roy Davidson'

Lungworts are very tough plants used as a groundcover for woodland gardens or border edging. Clump-forming and compact in habit with white-spotted foliage and light blue flowers in spring. Prefers fertile, well-drained, organic soil. Height: 20–30cm; width: 30–45cm. Shade to A.M. sun.

White Archangel
Lamium maculatum 'Anne Greenaway'

A wonderful groundcover for shady sites that is also tolerant of sun and poor soils. Spreading green foliage touched with chartreuse and silver displays mauve flowers in spring to summer. Prefers well-drained, moist soil. Height: 15–25cm; width: 60–100+cm. Shade to A.M. sun.

Trees

Russian Cypress
Microbiota decussata

This is a great evergreen groundcover that spreads indefinitely. We know of a 14-year-old shrub that was 4m wide! Bright green foliage turns purple-brown in winter. Requires moist soil to look its best. Height: 30cm; width: 3–4m. Shade to A.M. sun.

Sumac 'Gro-Low'
Rhus aromatica

Excellent for massing in beds or for erosion control. Compact, aromatic foliage displays yellow, scented blooms in late spring. Nice red fall colour. Height: 2–3 m; width: 2–3m. Sun to A.M. sun.

Sumac 'Gro-Low'

White Archangel 'Anne Greenaway'

Longleaf Lungwort 'Roy Davidson'

Pennisetum 'Rubrum' and 'Wave Pink' petunias combine to make a stunning summer show in planters and raised beds.

We have two 150cm, circular planters at the entrance to our front driveway. They are open to the ground, about 30cm high and are partially shaded in the morning and late afternoon. We like a variety of looks and are interested in trying to mix some permanent plantings in with our annual choices to make a bold statement. What grows here?

ONE OF THE BEST PLACES to make a strong design statement in the landscape is at an entrance. It is the first place a visitor sees and sets the tone for the rest of the garden. Any permanent plantings you choose should have more than one season of interest, including the consideration of form in winter. Play with bold-coloured annuals to create impact.

Annuals

Pennisetum 'Rubrum'

A great contrast plant that is superb in containers and flowerbeds. Rich burgundy, grassy foliage produces 30cm, spiked seed heads. Heat and drought tolerant. Height: 60–90cm; spacing: 45–75cm. Sun to P.M. sun.

Petunia 'Wave Pink'

Excellent in hanging baskets and containers or as an annual ground-cover. Bright fuchsia-pink, 5–7cm flowers on a variety that displays a superb branching and mounding habit. Weather tolerant. Height: 15cm; spreads to 120cm. Sun to P.M. sun.

Perennials

Daylily
Hemerocallis 'Exotic Love'

A clump-forming plant, ideal for any mixed border, producing golden-yellow flowers with a maroon eye and red edge in July. Divide every 3–5 years to maintain vigour. Prefers moist, fertile, well-drained soil. Height: 75cm; width: 45–75cm. Sun to P.M. sun.

Pennisetum 'Rubrum'

Daylily 'Exotic Love'

Evergreen Candytuft
Iberis sempervirens

This spreading plant with evergreen foliage has a sub-shrubby habit. In spring it produces white flowers that are sometimes flushed lilac. Trim off flowers after blooming is done and provide snow cover in winter. Thrives in well-drained, moist soil. Height: 15–30cm; width: 30–45cm. Sun to P.M. sun.

ROSES

David Thompson Explorer
Hybrid Rugosa

The least thorny of the Explorers. Although classed as medium red its showy double blooms are closer to a deep fuchsia and have a light fragrance. 7–8cm flowers bloom profusely July to frost. Height: 1m; spread: 1m. Sun.

TREES & SHRUBS

Caragana 'Weeping'
Caragana arborescens 'Pendula'

Great heat-tolerant feature plant in shrub beds or rockeries. Produces masses of yellow blooms in early summer on graceful, weeping branches. Height: graft dependent; width: 2–3m. Sun.

Juniper 'Mint Julep'—Pompon Form

Caragana 'Weeping'

Spruce 'Montgomery'

Juniper 'Mint Julep'
Spiral Form
Juniperus chinensis

Also known as 'Sea Green,' this juniper has brilliant mint-green foliage on a form that is spirally shaped. It requires annual shearing to maintain its unique shape. Height and spread: training dependent. Sun.

Juniper 'Mint Julep'
Pompon Form
Juniperus chinensis

Also known as 'Sea Green,' this is a unique and hardy feature plant with sheared balls of foliage that appear to float at different levels. Prune or shear annually to maintain this form. Height and spread: training dependent. Sun.

Pine 'Dwarf Globe'
Pinus sylvestris 'Glauca Nana'

A large, globe shape grafted onto a single stem, making a unique feature in shrub beds and rockeries. Prune annually to maintain form. Height and spread: training dependent. Sun.

Spruce 'Montgomery'
Picea pungens

Very attractive blue foliage on a compact feature plant that eventually grows into a broad, pyramidal shape. Height: 3m; width: 2–3m. Sun.

Juniper 'Mint Julep'—Spiral Form

Planters & Raised Beds

Evergreen Candytuft

Concrete and stone raised beds provide a good base, but it is the choice and placement of plants that will help define your gardening style.

We have a square, sunny patio that is surrounded by a raised bed made of stark, unattractive concrete blocks. This bed is about 60cm high and about 90cm wide. We want to fashion a classic look that includes some height. What grows here?

CREATE A FORMAL LOOK through symmetry and repetitive design. Place a tall plant in each corner of the planter with a different, shorter plant placed in each of the joining stretches. At regular intervals, incorporate trailing plants to hide the concrete blocks. As your planter is wide and open to the ground, consider hardy shrubs and perennials that normally wouldn't survive in a container, and those that won't get so tall as to block the scenery from a seated point of view.

ANNUALS

New Guinea Impatiens, Celebration Series
Very showy, mounding plants with attractive large blooms that stand out against glossy, medium to dark green foliage. Excellent in hanging baskets, containers or raised beds. Height: 30–35cm; spacing: 15–20cm. Sun.

Dracaena (Spike)
A good, frost-tolerant accent plant prized for its sturdy, grass-like foliage and tall, upright arching habit. Superb in containers and flowerbeds. It can be overwintered. Height: up to 90cm. Sun or shade.

Verbena, Aztec Series

Outstanding performance in hanging baskets, mixed planters and garden beds displaying large, bright, clustered flowers and a mounding and trailing growth habit. Height: up to 20cm; trails to 50cm. Sun.

PERENNIALS

Creeping Thyme
Thymus

Thick, green, aromatic foliage forms a dense, spreading mat that will spill over the planter's sides. Displays pink flowers in early summer. Tolerates poor, dry sites once established. Thrives in well-drained, neutral to alkaline soil. Height: 2–5cm; width: 30–60+cm. Sun to A.M. sun.

Dwarf Beebalm
Monarda 'Petite Delight'

A highly mildew-resistant, dwarf form for the front border, clump-forming in habit with aromatic foliage. Purple flowers bloom in late spring to early summer, attracting bees and hummingbirds. Prefers moist, moderately fertile, well-drained soil—avoid dry sites and winter wet. Height: 20–30cm; width: 30–40cm. Sun to P.M. sun.

ROSES

'Royal Edward' Explorer *Shrub*

An excellent border or groundcover rose that will soften the planter's edges. Hardy to Zone 3. Double, deep pink fading to medium pink, 5–6cm flowers bloom early summer through to frost in clusters of 1–7. Lightly fragrant. Height: 30–45cm; spread: 45–60cm. Sun.

'Winnipeg Parks' Parkland
Hardy Shrub

An absolutely lovely rose with almost fluorescent colour and a low, compact form. Hardy to Zone 2. Double, medium red, fading to dark red-pink on petal undersides, 7–9cm flowers bloom June to frost with a light fragrance. Height: 30–60cm; spread: 30–60cm. Sun.

TREES

Spiraea 'Golden Sparkling Carpet'
Spiraea

Little pink blooms. Striking, tiny, golden leaves on a carpet-forming shrub, rooting wherever branches contact the soil. Height: 15cm; width: 30cm. Sun.

Planters & Raised Beds

Creeping Thyme

It may seem simple, but a continuously blooming bed takes a lot of planning and consideration.

In one corner of our small front yard I've placed a slightly raised, kidney-shaped bed. I want to fill it with a small tree and some sun-loving plants that bloom throughout the spring and summer. What grows here?

GENERALLY SPEAKING, MOST trees, shrubs and perennials bloom for roughly a three-week period. Although there are exceptions to this rule, your choices are limited. It is better to approach the design of this bed considering successive blooming: one plant beginning to bloom as another finishes. Annuals and certain roses can be added to provide consistent colour throughout the growing months.

ANNUALS

Dahlia 'Harlequin Mix'
A traditional favourite that puts on a superb display in gardens and borders, featuring single-type, 6cm blooms with an inner collar of contrasting colour. Available in many two-toned, solid and bicoloured flowers—marvellous cutflowers. Height: 30cm; spacing: 15–20cm. Sun.

PERENNIALS

Carpathian Bellflower
Campanula carpatica 'Blue Clips'
A clump-forming, compact plant with bell-shaped, blue to violet flowers in summer. Deadhead to prolong blooming period. Prefers moist, fertile, well-drained soil. Height: 15–25cm; width: 30cm. Sun to P.M. sun.

Daylily
Hemerocallis 'Stella de Oro'

A short, clump-forming daylily that produces golden-yellow flowers continuously summer to fall. Its fragrant flowers last longer than a single day. Prefers moist, fertile, well-drained soil. Height: 30cm; width: 30–60cm. Sun to P.M. sun.

ROSES

'Henry Hudson' Explorer
Hybrid Rugosa

A prolific bloomer that is hardy to Zone 1. Double, apple blossom-white, 6-8cm flowers bloom June through summer with a gentle fragrance. Height: 60cm; spread: 90–100cm. Sun.

'Alexander Mackenzie' Explorer
Shrub

This variety displays a profusion of cup-shaped flowers in clusters of 6 to 12 and is hardy to Zone 1. Single, red, 6–7cm flowers bloom July to frost with a medium fragrance. Height: 2m; spread: 2m. Sun.

TREES

Willow 'Hakura Nishiki'
Salix integra 'Alba Maculata'

A very showy, fast-growing willow grafted to tree form with variegated, creamy-white and green foliage. A lovely feature plant in shrub beds. This hardy variety benefits from some wind protection and prefers moist soil. Prune annually. Height: graft dependent; width: 1.5–2m. Sun.

Planters & Raised Beds

Ornamental Crabapple 'Royal Beauty'
Malus

A spectacular ornamental, especially appropriate for a small yard. Deep greenish-purple-tinged foliage on a weeping form. Masses of pink blooms in late May and early June. Height: 4-5 m; Width: 3m. Sun.

Potentilla 'Goldstar'
Potentilla fruticosa

An upright form with masses of large, deep yellow blooms through summer. Very showy in beds or borders. Height: 90cm; width: 60–75cm. Sun to P.M. sun.

Rose 'Henry Hudson'

Potentilla 'Goldstar'

Carpathian Bellflower 'Blue Clips'

Willow 'Hakura Nishiki'

Selected Index

All plants are indexed by common name.
Perennials are also indexed by *Genus*.

About the Author

Inheriting his mother's love of horticulture, Jim Hole grew up gardening. After earning a Bachelor of Science in Agriculture with a major in plant science, Jim and his brother Bill helped develop Hole's Greenhouses & Gardens, which was founded by their parents Ted and Lois, into one of the largest retail greenhouse operations in Canada. Jim appears regularly on CBC radio and television call-in shows to share what he's learned from over 30 years of hands-on experience in the greenhouse.

Jim's interest has always centred on the science within the garden—explaining what makes plants tick with a clear and concise style, without losing sight of the beauty and wonder that makes gardening worthwhile.

Jim regularly contributes articles to several national magazines and writes a weekly gardening column for the *Edmonton Journal*. He is a frequent speaker at gardening groups and trade shows across North America. Jim is the co-author, with his mother Lois Hole, of five *Question & Answer* books and was the driving force behind the creation of *Lois Hole's Favorite Bulbs*.

For more from Jim Hole, including his speaking schedule, columns and gardening tips, visit www.enjoygardening.com.

❧

The success of this book is due entirely to the hard work of the staff of Hole's Greenhouses & Gardens over the years, including, but not limited to…

Gregory Brown	BOOK & COVER DESIGN
Christina McDonald & Earl J. Woods	CONTRIBUTING WRITERS
Bruce Timothy Keith, Christina McDonald, Dorothy Jedrasik & Jan Goodall	EDITORIAL COMMITTEE
Valerie Hole, Shane Neufeld & Bob Stadnyk	RESEARCH & CONSULTATION
Linda Affolder, Christina McDonald & Leslie Vermeer	EDITORS
Akemi Matsubuchi	PRINCIPAL PHOTOGRAPHY
Christina McDonald	PUBLICATION MANAGEMENT